Baking *for* Friends

Baking *for* Friends

Kathleen King

photographs by alexandra rowley

Distributed by Ingram Book Company. www.ingrambook.com

Project Manger: Michael Naimy
Editor: Rick Rodgers
Art Direction and Design: Barbara Scott-Goodman
Food Stylist: Liza Jernow
Prop Stylist: Pamela Duncan Silver

ISBN:978-0-578-10258-0

Manufactured in China

10 9 8 7 6 5 4 3 2 1

Tate's Bake Shop
62 Pine St.
East Moriches, NY 11940-1117
www.tatesbakeshop.com

For Fredis Guerra

Many thanks for your years of loyalty, dedication, and hard work

contents

introduction

Sharing happiness with the people I love has always been my wish as a baker, and *Baking for Friends* is inspired by that desire. I still get the same thrill from sharing my baked goods as I did when I started baking as a child on my parents' farmstead on Long Island—not far from where my bakery, Tate's Bake Shop, is located in Southampton, New York.

At just eleven years old, I began baking small batches of chocolate chip cookies in my mom's kitchen, which I sold to the neighbors off of a fold-out card table on the farm stand. I baked the kind of cookies I loved to eat: crunchy, chocolaty, and tinged with caramel. I called them "farm cookies." The process was simple, but I loved every minute of it. Soon I was selling more cookies than my dad, Tate, was selling eggs.

I loved to see the joy on people's faces as they bit into those cookies, surprised by their light crispness and smooth, buttery flavor. Those first happy bites were all the motivation I needed: I wanted to make a career out of spreading that joy. I suddenly had a new appreciation of what it meant to share—my baking became a new way of giving, a new way of connecting with people. And it was so much fun.

Scenes from the King family farm in Southampton, N.Y.
Above right: Kathleen and her dad, Tate.

Now, I love baking for the big events—the anniversaries, the birthdays, the holiday parties—but sometimes on any ordinary day, the mood just strikes, and I find myself in the kitchen, ready to bake. I love these spontaneous moments of inspiration, and when they happen to me, I find that I'm always baking with someone special in mind. I'll bake a delicious apple crisp and leave it on the doorstep of a neighbor, or if I'm having friends over on a Sunday afternoon, I'll have cookies baking in the oven for when my company arrives. I'll bake a cake and leave a slice I've wrapped up inside my friend's mailbox on my drive to work in the morning. My friends have started calling me "The Sugar Fairy." It's my way of spreading happiness.

Baking for Friends includes over 125 of my favorite desserts. You'll find recipes for scrumptious muffins and quick breads, perfect for nibbling with your morning coffee or tea; frosted layer cakes and cupcakes for holiday dinners and special occasions; fresh fruit pies for summer picnics and lunches with friends; plus cobblers, crisps, shortcakes, and more. All delicious, easy to bake, and very shareable.

If you're like me, you may have friends with dietary restrictions, which can range from simple preferences to food allergies and disorders. In these cases, it's good to have recipes on hand that are gluten-free, nut-free, low-fat, etc. I've included some of my favorite specialty recipes in *Baking for Friends*. I created these recipes for loved ones with dietary restrictions, and they've been tasted and approved by many of my friends with and without such restrictions. Because everyone deserves dessert.

I love the art and the craft of baking, but I would never spend all day making a single dessert. As you know, life can get hectic sometimes, and every baker wants to save time in the kitchen. After all, the easier the recipe, the more time you'll have to enjoy and share it. Here are some tips that anyone can use.

Make sure to stock your pantry with baking ingredients to save yourself a trip to the grocery store when a friend drops by unexpectedly, or when you simply find yourself in the mood to bake. Flour, cocoa, sweeteners, and flavorings can be stored for long periods, so

Left to right: Making Chubby Tate's; Tate's Bake Shop;
Kathleen with her best buddy, Yaffa.

have them on hand. Butter can be frozen for up to six months, so stock up when it's on sale. It's amazing how easy it is to make delicious baked goods with ingredients that you can easily find at your local supermarket, without a trip to the specialty shop. Occasionally, some of my recipes in *Baking for Friends* will call for an unusual ingredient, but trust me, there's always an easy-to-find substitute.

My freezer plays a big role in my baking—almost as much as my oven! Freezing prepped ingredients is a huge time-saver for those days when you're just too busy to bake a dessert in one go. Nuts can be toasted the day before baking, and streusel can be made and frozen in zip-tight bags. Rolled-out pie dough can be frozen right in the pie dish, so when it comes time to bake a pie for a friend, you're already halfway there. Some drop cookies (such as my Chubby Tates on page 111) can be shaped, wrapped, and frozen on a sheet pan. This way, you can bake the cookies as needed and serve them right out of the oven. Frozen cookie dough also helps with portion control: you can bake only a few cookies at a time if that's all you want.

Most importantly, don't be too concerned about making a picture-perfect dessert. I built Tate's Bake Shop on mouthwatering baked goods made with fresh, straight-forward ingredients. In my experience, most people prefer a simple treat that tastes wonderful rather than a complicated, extravagant dessert. It's all about the taste. The key to successful baking is just to enjoy it—don't fuss, don't stress, and don't try to make it "perfect." If you bake a delicious chocolate cake for a friend who loves chocolate, believe me, you won't be criticized for your frosting skills.

My approach to life is the same as my approach to baking—keep it simple. I enjoy taking long bicycle rides through the beautiful back roads of the Hamptons, walking my beloved dog, Yaffa, on the beach, spending time with my family, and of course, baking for friends.

This book is not only a collection of my recipes, it's also about sharing—connecting with the people in your life. Let them inspire you, and enjoy the process. They'll be able to taste the difference. Enjoy.

Kathleen King

✳ ✳

BAKING MY RECIPES

When it comes to baking, there are certain number of rules and techniques that should be adhered to, but don't let them keep you from enjoying yourself in the kitchen. Knowledge is power! Every baker has her or his way of doing things. Because these are my recipes, it might help you to know how I bake in my kitchen. Here are a few tips.

FLOUR

✳ I use unbleached all-purpose flour. It has not been treated with a bleaching agent, and so it is simply more natural and tastes better.

✳ When measuring dry ingredients, such as flour and sugar, I use the spoon-and-sweep method. Stir the ingredient to aerate it and spoon it into a measuring cup to overflowing. Using a knife, sweep off the excess so the ingredient is level with the rim of the cup. The alternate method, dip-and-sweep (dip the cup in the container of flour or sugar and then sweep) compacts the ingredient and increases its weight in the cup, which may affect your final results.

✳ If you are out of cake flour, use 14 tablespoons all-purpose flour for every cup of cake flour called for in the recipe. Or add 1 tablespoon cornstarch to a 1-cup measuring cup, spoon in all-purpose flour to fill the cup to overflowing, and level the flour.

✳ Almond flour is a great ingredient, adding a subtle nutty flavor to baked goods. It is available at natural food stores and many supermarkets. Make your own almond flour by pulsing natural sliced almonds in a food processor until they are very finely chopped. If the nuts seem to get oily during the chopping process, add a tablespoon or two of the recipe's flour or sugar to the food processor to help absorb the oil.

EGGS AND DAIRY

✳ Use Grade A large eggs. In some recipes, it is important to have the eggs at room temperature, so they incorporate easily into a batter or whip up better than cold eggs. Warm the chilled, uncracked eggs in a bowl of hot tap water for about 3 minutes before using.

✳ Although I usually prefer salted butter, you can use unsalted, adding salt at the rate of ¼ teaspoon for each 8 tablespoons (1 stick). However, do not substitute salted butter where I specify unsalted.

✳ Always use high-quality AA butter.

✳ ✳

✳ I use buttermilk a lot in my baking. Its acidity reacts with the gluten in flour to make tender baked goods. The problem is what to do with leftover buttermilk. So I admit that I usually use this easy substitute: For 1 cup buttermilk, add 1 tablespoon of cider or distilled white vinegar to a glass measuring cup and then add enough whole, low-fat, or skim milk to measure 1 cup. Let stand and curdle for 5 minutes.

✳ Have you run out of crème fraîche? Mix equal amounts of heavy cream and sour cream for a quick substitute.

✳ When measuring milk or another dairy product that will be mixed with another liquid, measure it into a large glass measuring cup, then add the other liquids and whisk to combine right in the cup. This saves a bowl and streamlines cleanup.

SUGAR AND SWEETENERS

✳ When measuring brown sugar, always pack it down firmly into the cup.

✳ When measuring sticky ingredients like honey, molasses, or corn syrup, spray the measuring cup with vegetable oil or heat it with hot water before adding the ingredient. The sticky ingredient will pour right out.

FLAVORINGS

✳ Store spices in a dark, cool place away from the stove, and use them within 6 months of purchase, so they aren't stale. Even though they may seem cheaper, spices (and, of course, dried herbs) sold in large containers can be wasteful if they lose their flavor before they are used up. I order my spices from Penzeys Spices (www.penzeys.com). They have a huge turnover so you know the products are fresh.

✳ Use only pure vanilla extract. It is more expensive than imitation extract, but you only use a small amount per recipe, and pure vanilla's aromatic flavor blends well with the other ingredients. My favorite is Madagascar Bourbon, which refers to where the beans are grown. I am not a fan of Mexican vanilla and never use it—I think it has a strong medicinal taste.

✳ Adjust recipes to your taste—start with the base batter or dough and make it your own. Leave out spices you don't like; add or omit nuts or change the type of nut; remove or add raisins; and substitute golden raisins or dried cranberries for dark raisins. Add semisweet, milk chocolate, or white chocolate chips, miniature or large.

✳ ✳

CHOCOLATE AND COCOA

✳ I like to bake with the full range of chocolate—milk, semisweet, bittersweet, white, and unsweetened. Sometimes I chose bitter-sweet over semisweet because of the former's stronger flavor. According to the FDA definition, all dark chocolates fall into the same category. The only way to tell if a chocolate is really bittersweet is to check the cacao percentage on the label. A truly bittersweet chocolate will have at least 62 to 70 percent cacao; chocolate with more than 62 percent cacao can make problems with some recipes, so don't go above that figure to be safe.

✳ Use a large chef's knife to chop chocolate for melting. The pieces should be the size of a dime or smaller. If you use a food processor, be careful, as the friction can soften some of the choc-olate. To melt chocolate, place it in a microwave-safe bowl. Microwave at Medium (50%) power for 30-second periods, stirring occasionally to check the progress of the melting, because the chocolate may hold its shape even if it is warm and almost melted. Pay attention to the process, and don't microwave for longer than 30 seconds at a time, or you could end up with a smoky mess.

✳ If you don't have a kitchen scale, you can estimate the ounces needed in a recipe by counting the indi-vidually wrapped squares of baking chocolate or using the scoring on a thin bar of eating chocolate to judge. While it isn't entirely accurate, you can also measure chopped chocolate by volume, figuring on 6 ounces of coarsely chopped chocolate per 1 cup.

✳ If you are out of unsweetened chocolate, you can substitute 3 tablespoons natural cocoa powder and 1 tablespoon vegetable oil per 1 ounce of chocolate.

✳ Cocoa powder comes in two varieties, natural and Dutch-processed. Natural cocoa powder is the familiar supermarket variety, such as Hershey's in the brown box. It is simply dried and pulverized cacao beans. This cocoa is acidic and reacts with the alkaline baking soda in a recipe to create the carbon dioxide that helps the cake or other baked goods rise. Dutch-processed cocoa has been treated with an alkali to reduce its acidity. It makes baked goods that are darker than those made with natural cocoa, and it does not react with baking soda. The two are not always interchangeable, so use what the recipes calls for, unless it says you can use either kind.

✱ ✱

TOASTING NUTS

✱   Toasting nuts really brings out their flavor, so do so whenever you have the time. Be sure to cool the nuts before adding them to the batter or dough. For a real time-saver, I toast nuts ahead of time and freeze them in zip-tight plastic bags.

✱   To toast almonds, walnuts, and pecans, spread the nuts out on a rimmed baking sheet in a single layer. Bake in a preheated 350°F oven, stirring occasionally, until they smell and look toasty, about 10 minutes. Let cool.

✱   To toast and skin hazelnuts, bake them for about 10 minutes, or until the skins crack. Wrap the nuts in a kitchen towel and rub off the skins with the towel. (Don't worry if some of the skins stay on.) Let cool on a plate.

EQUIPMENT

✱   I use 18-by-13-inch heavy-gauge aluminum rimmed baking sheets (also called half sheet pans). They hold a lot and their thickness discourages burning. Cookies in particular can burn if the pan is too thin, because the metal absorbs the heat too quickly and unevenly.

✱   Use an oven thermometer to double-check the accuracy of your oven: the thermostat is not enough. During preheating, put the thermometer in the center of a rack to get a good reading. Check it a couple of times, because the temperature changes as the heat source regulates high and low in order to achieve the average temperature. Then move the thermometer to the side of the rack to make room for the baked goods.

✱   Preheat the oven to the correct temperature and allow at least 15 minutes for most ovens to reach 350°F.

✱   All the recipes in this book were tested in a home oven. If you would like to use a convection oven, decrease the oven temperature by 25°F and bake for about one-third less time. I like convection baking because the fan in the oven provides even heat, but I don't use it when I'm recipe testing because most people don't have a convection oven.

✱   For most recipes, I use my 5-quart KitchenAid standing mixer. The Beater Blade, sold separately by an independent firm, is a redesign of the standard paddle attachment. I LOVE IT! This indispensible attachment mixes and scrapes down the bowl at the same time.

✱   Always use a timer—if you are like me and are constantly multitasking, it can be a lifesaver.

✱   I do a lot of baking at home, much more than we can eat, but it is just as easy to make a full batch of something as it is to make a small batch. So I freeze leftovers in zip-tight plastic bags, which gives me a supply of baked goods to share with friends or have ready for super-easy entertaining.

chapter 1

muffins, scones, & shortcakes

TIPS FOR MUFFINS AND SCONES

✳ When making muffins, mix the wet and dry ingredients just until moistened; the batter can still be somewhat lumpy. Overmixing will activate the gluten in the flour and make the muffins tough. The same goes for scones and quick breads. Truthfully, the only time I use an electric mixer to make muffins is to cream the butter and sugar together for recipes that require it. Stir in the dry ingredients by hand with a wooden spoon.

✳ If you have empty muffin cups in your batch, fill them with water before baking. This prevents the muffin pan from warping.

✳ In general, fill muffin cups just three-quarters full, to allow for the rising batter. However, depending on the recipe, the cups may be filled with more or less batter.

✳ When adding frozen fruit to batters, use IQF (individually quick frozen) fruit. Don't thaw it, or the softened fruit will discolor the batter. You may have to add a few more minutes to the baking time, because the frozen fruit may chill the batter.

✳ Freeze streusel crumbs for muffins, as well as for coffee cakes and pies, in zip-tight plastic bags until ready to use. If you bake often, this saves a lot of time.

✳ Use a ⅓-cup (about 3 ounces) food portion scoop, available at kitchen supply shops and online, to transfer muffin batter into the muffin cups.

apple crumb muffins

Makes 10 muffins

Don't let the long list of ingredients put you off. This muffin comes together quickly and is worth the few extra minutes.

Softened butter for the muffin cups

Crumb Topping

3 tablespoons unbleached
   all-purpose flour

2 tablespoons cold salted butter,
   cut into ½-inch cubes

2 tablespoons old-fashioned (rolled) oats

2 tablespoons firmly packed
   dark brown sugar

¼ teaspoon ground cinnamon

Muffins

1½ cups unbleached all-purpose flour

½ cup old-fashioned (rolled) oats

¼ cup granulated sugar

¼ cup firmly packed dark brown sugar

2 teaspoons baking powder

1¼ teaspoon ground cinnamon

½ teaspoon baking soda

½ teaspoon salt

¼ teaspoon freshly grated nutmeg

1 large apple, peeled, cored,
   and cut into ¼-inch dice (1¾ cups)

½ cup buttermilk

¼ cup applesauce

¼ cup vegetable oil

1 large egg plus 1 large egg yolk

2 teaspoons pure vanilla extract

1. Position an oven rack in the center of the oven and preheat the oven to 400°F. Butter ten 3-by-1 ½-inch muffin cups.

2. To make the crumb topping: In a small bowl, work together the flour, butter, oats, brown sugar and cinnamon with your fingertips until the mixture is crumbly.

3. To make the muffins: In a large bowl, whisk together the flour, oats, granulated sugar, brown sugar, baking powder, cinnamon, baking soda, salt, and nutmeg. Stir in the apple.

4. In a small bowl, whisk together the buttermilk, applesauce, vegetable oil, egg, yolk, and vanilla well. Pour over the apple mixture and stir just until combined. Do not overmix. Using a ⅓-cup food portion scoop or a spoon, transfer equal amounts of the batter into the prepared muffin cups. The cups will be full. Sprinkle the crumbs evenly on the muffins.

5. Bake until a wooden toothpick comes out clean when inserted in the middle of a muffin, about 20 minutes. Let the muffins cool in the pan on a wire cooling rack for 10 to 15 minutes. Remove from the pan and let cool completely on the rack.

lemon-poppy seed muffins

Makes 10 muffins

This recipe was given to me over twenty-five years ago by one of my oldest, most convivial customers who liked to tell me about his collection of cookbooks. One day, I did have an opportunity to visit his apartment in the city, where, true to his word, he had hundreds of books! This lemony, moist muffin was the most requested by my son, Justin, when he was in high school.

Softened butter for the muffin cups

2½ cups unbleached all-purpose flour

¾ cup plus 1 teaspoon sugar

3 tablespoons poppy seeds

2 teaspoons baking powder

1 teaspoon salt

¼ teaspoon baking soda

8 tablespoons (1 stick) salted butter, cut into tablespoons

Grated zest of 2 lemons

½ cup freshly squeezed lemon juice

2 large eggs, lightly beaten

½ cup sour cream (not low-fat)

1. Position an oven rack in the center of the oven and preheat the oven to 400°F. Butter ten 3-by-1½-inch muffin cups.

2. In a large bowl, whisk together the flour, ¾ cup of the sugar, the poppy seeds, baking powder, salt, and baking soda.

3. In a small saucepan, melt the butter. Remove from the heat. Stir in the lemon zest and juice, then the eggs, and whisk until well blended. Whisk in the sour cream. Pour into the flour mixture and fold together just until combined. Do not overmix. Using a ⅓-cup food portion scoop or a spoon, transfer the batter into the prepared muffin cups. Sprinkle the tops with the remaining 1 teaspoon sugar.

4. Bake until a wooden toothpick inserted in center of a muffin comes out clean, 15 to 18 minutes. Let the muffins cool in the pan on a wire cooling rack for 10 minutes. Remove from the pan and let cool completely on the rack.

banana mocha muffins

Makes 12 muffins

This muffin recipe was published in the Family Circle *magazine years ago when they did a story about the Bake Shop. I had almost forgotten about it until I got a request from a woman who had lost the recipe. Her family was upset with her and she needed it back! Thank you for bringing this back to my kitchen.*

Softened butter for the muffin cups

2½ cups unbleached all-purpose flour

1 teaspoon baking powder

½ teaspoon baking soda

½ teaspoon salt

1 tablespoon instant coffee powder or
 1½ teaspoons instant espresso powder

1 tablespoon boiling water

1⅓ cups mashed fully ripe bananas
 (about 3 bananas)

1¼ cups sugar

½ pound (2 sticks) salted butter,
 at room temperature, plus more
 for the muffin cups

1 large egg, at room temperature

1 cup (6 ounces) semisweet chocolate chips

1. Position an oven rack in the center of the oven and preheat the oven to 400°F. Butter twelve 3-by-1½-inch muffin cups.

2. In a large bowl, whisk together the flour, baking powder, baking soda, and salt. In a medium bowl, dissolve the instant coffee in the water. Add the bananas and stir well.

3. In a large bowl, beat the sugar and butter with an electric mixer set on high speed until light and fluffy, about 3 minutes. Beat in the egg, then the banana mixture. Using a wooden spoon, stir in the flour mixture just until combined. Do not overmix. Fold in the chocolate chips. Using a ⅓-cup food portion scoop or a spoon, transfer the batter to the prepared muffin cups.

4. Bake until a wooden toothpick inserted in center of a muffin comes out clean, 25 to 30 minutes. Let the muffins cool in the pan on a wire cooling rack for 10 minutes. Remove the muffins from the pan and let cool completely on the rack.

peach muffins

Makes 15 muffins

I recently stopped by my family farm, North Sea Farms, for some fresh vegetables and chicken. When I was leaving, one of the sales staff asked if I could use a case of bruised peaches. I thought, "I really don't have time for more work right now," but I couldn't see them going to waste. I decided to start with this simple muffin, which is full of spicy peach sweetness. The rest, I thought, would find themselves in a pie and cobbler, maybe for the shop, maybe for a friend.

Softened butter for the muffin cups

3 cups unbleached all-purpose flour

¾ cup sugar

1 tablespoon baking powder

1 teaspoon ground cinnamon

½ teaspoon baking soda

½ teaspoon salt

1¼ cups buttermilk

2 large eggs

1 tablespoon pure vanilla extract

12 tablespoons (1½ sticks)
  salted butter, melted

2 large ripe peaches, peeled, pitted,
  and cut into ½-inch dice (2 cups)

1. Position an oven rack in the center of the oven and preheat the oven to 400°F. Butter fifteen 3-by-1½-inch muffin cups.

2. In a large bowl, whisk together the flour, sugar, baking powder, cinnamon, baking soda, and salt. In a medium bowl, whisk together the buttermilk, eggs, and vanilla. Whisk in the melted butter. Pour into the flour mixture and mix just until combined. Do not overmix. Fold in the peaches. Using a ⅓-cup food portion scoop or a spoon, transfer the batter into the prepared muffin cups.

3. Bake until a wooden toothpick inserted in the center of a muffin comes out clean, about 25 minutes. Let the muffins cool in the pan on a wire cooling rack for 10 minutes. Remove from the pan and let cool completely on the rack.

ginger plum muffins

Makes 13 muffins

Every autumn, quarts of prune plums appear in local markets. They are a very versatile and firm-textured fruit that I always look forward to. The plums add a nice tart contrast to the sweet muffins, which can be served as dessert with ice cream or spiced whipped cream.

Softened butter for the muffin cups

3 cups unbleached all-purpose flour

¾ cup firmly packed dark brown sugar

1 tablespoon baking powder

2 teaspoons ground ginger

½ teaspoon baking soda

¾ teaspoon salt

1¼ cups milk

12 tablespoons (1½ sticks) salted butter, melted

2 large eggs

2 teaspoons pure vanilla extract

Grated zest of ½ orange

10 prune plums, pitted and diced (1¾ cups)

¼ cup finely chopped crystallized ginger

1. Position an oven rack in the center of the oven and preheat the oven to 400°F. Butter twelve 3-by-1½-inch muffin cups and 1 ramekin of about the same size.

2. In a large bowl, whisk together the flour, brown sugar, baking powder, ground ginger, baking soda, and salt. In a small bowl, whisk together the milk, melted butter, eggs, vanilla, and orange zest. Pour into the flour mixture and stir just until combined. Do not overmix. Fold in the plums and crystallized ginger. Using a ⅓-cup food portion scoop or spoon, transfer the batter into the prepared muffin cups.

3. Bake until a wooden toothpick comes out clean when inserted into the center of the muffin, about 25 minutes. Let the muffins cool in the pan on a wire cooling rack for 10 minutes. Remove from the pan and serve warm, or let cool completely on the rack.

irish soda bread muffins

Makes 10 muffins

St. Patrick's Day is always a great excuse to make Irish soda bread. Most people love it but limit themselves to the holiday only. Making the soda bread in muffin form makes it more of an everyday treat and the muffins also develop a very tasty, crisp bottom and a nice craggy top, which makes it hard to eat just one. These are best served the day they are baked. Since they are so quick, make them for breakfast, or serve them with the traditional St. Patrick's Day corned beef dinner, right from the oven.

Softened butter for the muffin cups

2 cups unbleached all-purpose flour

¼ cup sugar

1½ teaspoons baking powder

½ teaspoon baking soda

½ teaspoon salt

4 tablespoons (½ stick) cold unsalted butter, cut into ½-inch cubes

½ cup dried currants

1 teaspoon caraway seeds (optional)

1 cup buttermilk

1. Position an oven rack in the center of the oven and preheat the oven to 375°F. Butter ten 3-by-1½-inch muffin cups.

2. In a medium bowl, whisk together the flour, sugar, baking powder, baking soda, and salt. Using a pastry blender or fork, cut in the butter until the mixture resembles coarse meal with some pea-sized pieces. Add the currants and the caraway, if using, and toss to coat with the flour mixture. Stir in the buttermilk and mix just until combined into a stiff dough.

3. Using ⅓-cup food portion scoop or two spoons, spoon the dough into the muffin cups. (It is stiff and will not flow like typical muffin batter.) Using scissors, snip an X in the top of each muffin. (The X will disappear during baking, but it makes the tops craggier and less even.)

4. Bake until the muffin tops are golden brown and spring back when pressed with a fingertip, 20 to 25 minutes. Remove from the pan and let cool on a wire cooling rack for 5 minutes. Serve warm.

hot cross muffins

Makes 12 muffins

While walking on the beach with my friend Judith Anne, I was discussing my recipe of the month for our website and that I hadn't decided on one that would suit the Easter holidays. She said, "Hot cross buns!" and before we knew it, the recipe was developed, a quick and easy muffin with golden raisins and cranberries. When I got home, I put together these muffins, which are similar in flavor to the traditional sweet yeast bun, but less time consuming to make. The muffins are moist and keep well.

Muffins
Softened butter for the muffin cups
2 cups unbleached all-purpose flour
½ cup granulated sugar
1 tablespoon baking powder
Grated zest of ½ orange
Grated zest of 1 lemon
½ teaspoon salt
¼ teaspoon ground cinnamon
⅛ teaspoon ground allspice

1 cup mixed dried currants, dried cranberries, and golden raisins, in any combination
1 cup milk
8 tablespoons (1 stick) salted butter, melted
1 large egg
1 teaspoon pure vanilla extract

Icing
½ cup confectioners' sugar, sifted
1 tablespoon fresh lemon juice

1. Position an oven rack in the center of the oven and preheat the oven to 400°F. Butter twelve 3-by-1½-inch muffin cups.

2. To make the muffins: In a large bowl, whisk together the flour, sugar, baking powder, orange and lemon zests, salt, cinnamon, and allspice. Add the dried fruit and mix with your fingers, breaking apart any fruit that is stuck together.

3. In a small bowl, whisk together the milk, melted butter, egg, and vanilla. Pour into the dry ingredients and stir just until combined. Do not overmix. Using a ⅓-cup food portion scoop or a spoon, transfer the batter into the prepared muffin cups.

4. Bake until a wooden toothpick inserted into the center of a muffin comes out clean. (These muffins will be flat on top, without the traditional hump.) Let the muffins cool in the pan on a wire cooling rack for 10 minutes. Remove from the pan and let cool completely on the rack.

5. To make the icing: In a small bowl, mix together the confectioners' sugar and lemon juice to make a loose icing. Scrape the icing into a small zip-tight plastic bag, squeeze it into a bottom corner of the bag, and snip off the corner of the bag. Pipe a cross on top of each cooled muffin. Let stand until the icing sets.

pumpkin muffins

Makes 12 muffins

In the fall, I yearn for the flavors of pumpkin, spices, sweet potatoes, and maple syrup. This muffin is moist, spicy, full of raisins and walnuts, and especially good with a cup of hot tea in the late afternoon. For a yummy quick spread, mix some cream cheese with maple syrup.

Softened butter for the muffin cups

2 cups unbleached all-purpose flour

½ cup firmly packed dark brown sugar

1½ teaspoons baking powder

1 teaspoon ground cinnamon

½ teaspoon ground cloves

½ teaspoon salt

¼ teaspoon freshly grated nutmeg

¼ teaspoon baking soda

1 cup solid-pack pumpkin (not pumpkin pie filling)

8 tablespoons (1 stick) salted butter, melted

¾ cup chopped walnuts

2 large eggs

¼ cup plain low-fat yogurt

¼ cup Grade B pure maple syrup

1 teaspoon vanilla extract

¾ cup dark raisins or dried cranberries

1. Position an oven rack in the center of the oven and preheat the oven to 400°F. Butter twelve 3-by-1½-inch muffin cups.

2. In a large bowl, whisk together the flour, brown sugar, baking powder, cinnamon, cloves, salt, nutmeg, and baking soda. In another large bowl, whisk together the pumpkin, melted butter, eggs, yogurt, maple syrup, and vanilla. Pour into the flour mixture and mix just until combined. Do not overmix. Fold in the raisins and walnuts. Using a ⅓-cup food portion scoop or spoon, transfer the batter to the prepared muffin cups.

3. Bake until a wooden toothpick inserted in center of a muffin comes out clean, 25 to 30 minutes. Let the muffins cool in the pan on a wire cooling rack for 10 minutes. Remove from the pan and cool completely on the rack.

chocolate chip muffins

Makes 12 muffins

These muffins are outrageous warm from the oven, but still delicious at room temperature. Kids love them.

Softened butter for the muffin cups

2 cups unbleached all-purpose flour

1 tablespoon baking powder

1 teaspoon baking soda

½ teaspoon salt

1 cup granulated sugar

6 tablespoons (¾ stick) salted butter, at room temperature

1 large egg, at room temperature

1 teaspoon pure vanilla extract

1¼ cups sour cream (not low-fat)

1 cup (6 ounces) semisweet chocolate chips

2 tablespoons raw or granulated sugar mixed with ¼ teaspoon ground cinnamon (optional)

1. Position an oven rack in the center of the oven and preheat the oven to 400°F. Butter twelve 3-by-1½-inch muffin cups.

2. In a medium bowl, whisk together the flour, baking powder, baking soda, and salt. In a large bowl, beat the sugar and butter with an electric mixer set on high speed until combined, about 1 minute. Beat in the egg and vanilla. Scrape down the sides of the bowl. Beat in the sour cream. Using a wooden spoon, stir in the flour mixture, just until combined. Do not overmix. Fold in the chocolate chips. Using a ⅓-cup food portion scoop or a spoon, transfer equal amounts of the batter into the prepared muffin cups. Sprinkle with the cinnamon sugar, if desired.

3. Bake until the muffins are golden brown and the centers spring back when touched, about 20 minutes. Let the muffins cool in the pans on a wire cooling rack for 10 minutes. Remove from the pan and let cool completely on the rack.

rocky road muffins

Makes 12 muffins

Rich, chocolaty, and gooey, this treat is almost like an undressed cupcake. Line the cups with paper liners, or the marshmallows will stick.

3 ounces unsweetened chocolate, finely chopped

6 tablespoons (¾ stick) salted butter, cut into tablespoons

1½ cups unbleached all-purpose flour

½ cup firmly packed dark brown sugar

¼ cup almond flour (or natural sliced almonds very finely chopped in a food processor)

¼ cup natural cocoa powder

1 tablespoon baking powder

½ teaspoon baking soda

¼ teaspoon salt

1 cup mini marshmallows or quartered large ones

¾ cup semisweet chocolate chips

1¼ cups buttermilk

1 large egg

2 teaspoons pure vanilla extract

½ cup toasted and coarsely chopped blanched or natural almonds

1. Position an oven rack in the center of the oven and preheat the oven to 375°F. Line twelve 3-by-1½-inch muffin cups with paper liners.

2. In a microwave oven on Medium (50%), in a microwave-safe bowl, heat the chocolate and butter together, stirring occasionally, until just melted, about 2 minutes. (Or melt the chocolate and butter together in a medium saucepan over low heat, stirring often.)

3. In a large bowl, whisk together the flour, brown sugar, almond flour, cocoa powder, baking powder, baking soda, and salt, making sure that there are no lumps of brown sugar. Add the marshmallows and ½ cup of the chocolate chips to the flour mixture and toss to coat.

4. In a large glass measuring cup, whisk together the buttermilk, egg, and vanilla. Add the chocolate mixture to the flour mixture, followed by the buttermilk mixture, and stir just until combined. Using a ⅓-cup food portion scoop or a spoon, transfer the batter to the prepared muffin cups; the cups will be full. Sprinkle the almonds and remaining ¼ cup chocolate chips on top of the muffins.

5. Bake until a wooden toothpick inserted into the center of a muffin comes out clean, about 20 minutes. Let the muffins cool in the pan on a wire cooling rack for 15 minutes. These are heavenly warm and equally delicious at room temperature.

rhubarb swirl rolls

Makes 9 rolls

Pouring syrup over the rolls creates a coating that clings to the bottom of each serving. Make sure the rhubarb is minced, or the rolls will not bake properly.

Softened butter for the pan

Syrup
¼ cup sugar
¼ teaspoon cornstarch
¼ cup water
1 teaspoon salted butter
½ teaspoon pure vanilla extract

Dough
2 cups unbleached all-purpose flour
2 teaspoons baking powder

¼ teaspoon salt
4 tablespoons (½ stick) cold salted butter, cut into ½-inch cubes
1 cup heavy cream

Filling
4 tablespoons (½ stick) salted butter, at room temperature
½ cup sugar
½ teaspoon ground cinnamon
¼ teaspoon freshly grated nutmeg
2 cups minced rhubarb

1. Position an oven rack in the center of the oven and preheat the oven to 375°F. Lightly butter a 9-inch square baking pan.

2. To make the syrup: In a small saucepan, mix the sugar and cornstarch. Stir in the water and bring to a boil over medium heat, stirring often. Add the butter and boil for about 1 minute, until the syrup is slightly thickened. Remove from the heat and stir in the vanilla.

3. To make the dough: In a medium bowl, whisk together the flour, baking powder, and salt. Work in the cold butter with a pastry blender or your fingertips until the mixture is crumbly with some pea-sized pieces. Add the cream and stir just until combined. Turn the dough out onto a lightly floured board and knead a few times. Roll the dough into a 12-by-9-inch rectangle about ¼ inch thick.

4. Spread the softened butter evenly over dough. In a bowl, mix together the sugar, cinnamon, and nutmeg. Stir in the rhubarb. Distribute evenly over the dough. Immediately, starting from a long side, roll up the dough tightly. Cut into 9 equal slices. Arrange the slices cut sides up in the prepared pan. Drizzle the syrup evenly over the slices.

5. Bake until the tops are beginning to brown, about 45 minutes. Let cool in the pan for 15 minutes. Remove from the pan and serve warm.

maple, bacon, and date scones

Makes 16 scones

When I first saw a bacon chocolate bar at the Fancy Food Show in New York City, I started thinking of endless combinations of bacon and sweets. This scone is a perfect breakfast treat—it tastes like pancakes and bacon in just one bite.

1¾ cups whole wheat flour

1½ cups unbleached all-purpose flour

¼ cup firmly packed dark brown sugar

1 tablespoon baking powder

½ teaspoon baking soda

½ teaspoon salt

10 tablespoons (1¼ sticks) cold salted butter, cut into ½-inch cubes

1½ cups pitted and chopped dates

12 ounces sliced bacon, cut into ½-inch-wide pieces, cooked until crisp, drained, and cooled

1 cup buttermilk

⅓ cup plus 1 tablespoon Grade B pure maple syrup

1 large egg

2 tablespoons Demerara or other raw sugar

1. Position oven racks in the top third and center of the oven and preheat the oven to 400°F. Line 2 large rimmed baking sheets with parchment paper or silicone baking mats.

2. To make the scones: In a large bowl, whisk together the whole wheat and all-purpose flours, brown sugar, baking powder, baking soda, and salt. Using a pastry blender or your fingertips, cut in the butter until the mixture is crumbly with some pea-sized pieces of butter. Add the dates and toss to coat with the flour mixture. Repeat with the bacon. Whisk the buttermilk and ⅓ cup of maple syrup together in a measuring cup. Pour into the flour mixture and stir just until combined. Do not overmix.

3. Turn the dough out onto a lightly floured work surface and knead a few times. Roll out into a 1-inch-thick round. Using a 2½-inch round cookie cutter, pressing firmly to cut through the dates, cut out the scones as close together as possible to avoid excess scraps. Arrange at least 2 inches apart on the prepared baking sheets. Gently press the scraps together, roll out again, and cut more scones.

4. In a small bowl, whisk together the egg and remaining 1 tablespoon maple syrup. Brush the tops of the scones lightly with the egg mixture and sprinkle with the Demerara sugar.

5. Bake, switching the positions of the baking sheets from top to bottom and front to back halfway through baking, until the scones are golden brown, about 20 minutes. Let cool on the pans for 10 minutes. Serve warm.

cinnamon swirl scones

Makes 12 rolls

This is a scone dough filled, rolled up, and sliced like a cinnamon bun. The scones are much quicker than traditional yeast rolls, but equally delicious.

Filling

8 tablespoons (1 stick) salted butter, at room temperature

½ cup firmly packed dark brown sugar

1 tablespoon ground cinnamon

Dough

4 cups unbleached all-purpose flour

⅓ cup granulated sugar

2 tablespoons baking powder

½ teaspoon salt

8 tablespoons (1 stick) cold salted butter, cut into ½-inch cubes

1 cup dark raisins

1¾ cups half-and-half

Icing

½ cup confectioners' sugar, sifted

1 tablespoon plus 1 teaspoon water

1. Position the oven racks in the top third and center of the oven and preheat the oven to 375°F. Line 2 large rimmed baking sheets with parchment paper or silicone baking mats.

2. To make the filling: In a small bowl, mix the butter, brown sugar, and cinnamon until smooth.

3. To make the dough: In a large bowl, whisk together the flour, sugar, baking powder, and salt. Using a pastry blender or your fingertips, work in the butter until the mixture is crumbly with some pea-sized pieces of butter. Do not overmix. Mix in the raisins. Stir in the half-and-half and mix just until the dry ingredients are moistened.

4. On a lightly floured work surface, roll out the dough into a 17-by-12-inch rectangle about ¼ inch thick. Spread the cinnamon filling evenly over the top of dough, leaving a ½-inch border on all four sides. Starting at a long side, tightly roll the dough up into a log. Cut the dough into 2-inch slices and arrange them, cut sides up, 4 inches apart on the prepared baking sheets.

5. Bake, switching the positions of the baking sheets from front to back and top to bottom halfway through baking, until the rolls are slightly golden, 25 to 30 minutes. Let cool on the pans for 10 minutes.

6. To make the icing: In a small bowl, mix the confectioners' sugar and water with a fork until smooth. Drizzle over the buns. Serve warm, or let cool to room temperature.

raspberry chocolate scones

Makes 6 large scones

I tested this recipe a few times to get a scone with melting chocolate, tart raspberries, a hint of orange, a moist interior, and a crispy top.

Scones

2 cups unbleached all-purpose flour

½ cup firmly packed dark brown sugar

¼ cup almond flour (or natural sliced almonds very finely chopped in a food processor)

2 teaspoons baking powder

¼ teaspoon baking soda

¼ teaspoon salt

8 tablespoons (1 stick) cold salted butter, cut into ½-inch cubes

¾ cup IQF (individually quick frozen) raspberries, not thawed

½ cup semisweet chocolate chips

Grated zest of 1 orange

⅔ cup buttermilk

Topping

1 large egg

1 tablespoon granulated sugar

¼ cup sliced natural almonds (optional)

1. Position the oven racks in the top third and center of the oven and preheat the oven to 400°F. Line 1 large rimmed baking sheet with parchment paper or a silicone baking mat.

2. To make the scones: In a large bowl, whisk together the flour, brown sugar, almond flour, baking powder, baking soda, and salt. Work in the butter with a pastry blender or your fingertips until the mixture is crumbly with some pea-sized pieces of butter.

3. Add the raspberries, chocolate chips and orange zest to the flour mixture and toss to coat. Add the buttermilk and stir just until combined.

4. Turn the dough out onto a generously floured work surface and gently knead a few times. Pat the dough into an 1-inch-thick round.

5. Cut like a pizza into 6 equal wedges, and separate the wedges. Arrange 1 inch apart on the prepared baking sheet.

6. To make the topping: In a small bowl, whisk together the egg and sugar. Lightly brush the top of each wedge with the egg mixture, and sprinkle with an equal amount of almonds, if using.

7. Bake until the tops of the scones are golden brown and the centers feel firm when pressed with your fingertip, about 30 minutes. Let cool slightly on the pan. Serve warm.

pumpkin pie scones

Makes 15 scones

My sister invented these scones, which are moistened with the pumpkin pie filling on page 81. See the make-ahead instructions below to be able to make them on a busy holiday morning. Try to serve these with Miss Amy's Apple Butter (www.missamys.com).

4 cups unbleached all-purpose flour

⅓ cup firmly packed dark brown sugar

2 tablespoons baking powder

½ teaspoon salt

8 tablespoons (1 stick) cold salted butter, cut into ½-inch cubes

¾ cup dried cranberries

¼ cup chopped crystallized ginger

2 cups filling from Two-Recipe Pumpkin Pie (page 81)

2 tablespoons heavy cream

2 tablespoons Demerara or other raw sugar

1. Position the oven racks in the top third and center of the oven and preheat the oven to 375°F. Line 2 large rimmed baking sheets with parchment paper or silicone baking mats.

2. In the bowl of a heavy-duty standing electric mixer, whisk together the flour, brown sugar, baking powder, and salt. Add the butter. Fit the mixer with the paddle attachment and mix on medium-low speed until the mixture is crumbly with some pea-sized pieces of butter. With the mixer on low speed, add the dried cranberries and ginger. Add the pumpkin pie filling and mix just until combined. Do not overmix.

3. On a lightly floured work surface, roll the dough out into an 1-inch-thick round. Using a 3-inch round cookie cutter lightly dipped in flour, cut out the scones as close together as possible to avoid excess scraps. Arrange the scones about 2 inches apart on the prepared baking sheets. Gently press the scraps together, roll out again, and cut more. Brush the tops of the scones lightly with the cream and sprinkle with the Demerara sugar.

4. Bake, switching the position of the baking sheets from top to bottom and front to back halfway through baking, until the scones are golden brown and spring back when pressed with a fingertip, about 30 minutes. Let cool slightly, and serve warm.

Make-Ahead Instructions: The night before baking, mix the dry ingredients and cut in the butter. Make the pumpkin pie filling. Transfer each to its own zip-tight plastic bag and refrigerate. The next day, preheat the oven. Stir 2 cups of the pumpkin pie filling into the dry ingredient and shape and bake the scones. (Bake the Two-Recipe Pumpkin Pie with the remaining filling.)

chocolate shortcakes

Makes 20 shortcakes

I set out to make chocolate shortcakes for my friend Jane LaGuardia's birthday, but I improvised by serving chocolate whoopie pie cakes from the Bake Shop with fruit and whipped cream. When I had more time, I came up with this keeper. Chocolate shortcake is decadent served with a mix of fresh strawberries and raspberries and, of course, whipped cream. Make them ahead and freeze to have on hand for when friends call unexpectedly.

3¼ cups unbleached all-purpose flour

1 cup firmly packed dark brown sugar

¾ cup Dutch-processed cocoa powder

2 tablespoons baking powder

½ teaspoon salt

8 tablespoons (1 stick) cold salted butter, cut into ½-inch cubes

1 cup (6 ounces) semisweet chocolate chips

2 cups heavy cream

1 teaspoon pure vanilla extract

1 large egg beaten with 1 tablespoon Demerara or other raw sugar, or sanding sugar, for glazing

1. Position the oven racks in the top third and center of the oven and preheat the oven to 375°F. Line 2 large rimmed baking sheets with parchment paper or silicone baking mats.

2. In a large bowl, stir together the flour, brown sugar, cocoa powder, baking powder, and salt. Using a pastry blender or your fingertips, cut in the butter until the mixture is crumbly with some pea-sized bits of butter. Mix in the chocolate chips. Add the cream and vanilla and stir vigorously for 10 seconds.

3. On a lightly floured work surface, roll the dough out into a round about 1 inch thick. Using a 2½-inch round cookie cutter lightly dipped in flour, cut out the shortcakes, cutting them as close together as possible to avoid excess scraps. Arrange the shortcakes about 3 inches apart on the prepared baking sheets. Gently press the scraps into together, roll out again, and cut out more shortcakes. Brush the tops lightly with the egg glaze.

4. Bake, switching the position of the baking sheets from top to bottom and front to back halfway through baking, until the shortcakes have risen and are golden brown, about 25 minutes. Serve warm or let cool, wrap, and freeze for up to 1 month.

star-shaped blueberry shortcakes

Makes 10 to 11 shortcakes

This shortcake/scone can be made round and served warm with butter, as you would any scone, but I decided to do it in a star shape because it is more fun as a Fourth of July dessert, served with fresh raspberries and whipped cream. These are delicious and very festive!

2 cups unbleached all-purpose flour

¼ cup sugar, plus 1 teaspoon
 for sprinkling

1 tablespoon baking powder

¼ teaspoon salt

Grated zest of 1 lemon

4 tablespoons (½ stick) cold salted butter
 cut into ½-inch cubes

1 cup heavy cream, plus 2 teaspoons
 for brushing

1 cup fresh blueberries

1. Position an oven rack in the center of the oven and preheat the oven to 400°F. Line a large rimmed baking sheet with parchment paper or a silicone baking mat.

2. In a large bowl, whisk together the flour, the ¼ cup sugar, baking powder, salt, and lemon zest. Using a pastry blender or your fingertips, work in the butter until the mixture is crumbly with some pea-sized pieces of butter. Add the 1 cup of heavy cream and stir just the dry ingredients are moistened and combined. Do not overmix.

3. On a lightly floured work surface, roll out the dough into a 1-inch-thick rectangle. Spread the blueberries evenly on top of dough. Gently work the dough into a ball, being careful not to crush the berries, and roll the dough out again into a 1-inch-thick rectangle.

4. Using a 3-inch star cookie or biscuit cutter dipped in flour, cut out the shortcakes, cutting them as close together as possible to avoid excess scraps. Arrange the shortcakes about 3 inches apart on the prepared baking sheet. Gently press the scraps together, roll out again, and cut more stars. Using a pastry brush, lightly brush the tops of the shortcakes with the remaining 2 teaspoons cream and sprinkle with the remaining 1 teaspoon sugar.

5. Bake until the shortcakes are golden brown and feel somewhat firm when the tops are pressed with a fingertip, 25 to 30 minutes. Serve warm, or let cool to room temperature.

chapter 2

tea loaves
& quick breads

TIPS FOR TEA LOAVES AND QUICK BREADS

✳ Many loaf pans and fluted tube pans have dark nonstick surfaces, which absorb heat in the oven (shiny surfaces reflect the heat) and cook the batter more quickly. If you use nonstick pans, check to be sure that the baked goods aren't browning too rapidly. If they are, reduce the oven temperature by 25°F. Then check for doneness about 10 minutes before the end of the estimated baking time.

✳ Are you afraid that your tea loaf will stick to the pan? Always line the pan bottom with parchment or waxed paper, and you will never have a problem.

✳ To prevent a dark rim from forming at the edges of quick breads, butter the loaf pan on the bottom and only halfway up the sides.

✳ Never put a Bundt pan on a baking sheet: the tube in the middle of the pan must get hot so the wide cake will bake properly. A baking sheet would block the heat and keep it from properly circulating into the tube.

✳ Use a thin bamboo skewer to test Bundt cakes and loaves; a toothpick is not long enough.

chocolate-pear tea bread

Makes 10 servings

I think chocolate goes with almost any fruit. This pear tea bread really took off when I added chocolate chunks. The flavors of the brown sugar and butter really come through and there is just enough chocolate to not overpower the delicate pears.

Softened butter for the pan

1¾ cups unbleached all-purpose flour

2 teaspoons baking powder

½ teaspoon salt

8 tablespoons (1 stick) salted butter, at room temperature

¾ cup firmly packed dark brown sugar

2 large eggs, at room temperature

½ cup applesauce

2 teaspoons pure vanilla extract

2 ripe Anjou pears, peeled, cored, and diced (about 2 cups)

1 cup (6 ounces) semisweet chocolate chunks or chips

1. Position an oven rack in the center of the oven and preheat the oven to 350°F. Lightly butter a 9-by-5-by-3-inch loaf pan. Line the bottom of the pan with parchment or waxed paper.

2. In a medium bowl, whisk together the flour, baking powder, and salt. In a large bowl, beat the butter and brown sugar with an electric mixer set on high speed until light and fluffy, about 3 minutes. One at a time, beat in the eggs, scraping down the sides of the bowl as needed. Mix in the applesauce and vanilla. With the mixer on low speed, gradually beat in the flour mixture, and mix just until smooth, scraping down the bowl as needed. Fold in the pears and chocolate chunks. Spread the batter in the prepared pan.

3. Bake until a bamboo skewer inserted in the center of the cake comes out clean, about 1 hour. Let cool in the pan on a wire cooling rack for 10 minutes. Invert the cake onto the rack and unmold. Remove the paper, turn the loaf right side up, and let cool completely.

white chocolate cranberry bread

Makes 10 servings

This is a beautiful quick bread with bright, tart cranberries and the sweetness of white choco-late. Melt high-quality white chocolate (look for cocoa butter in the ingredients) to flavor the batter, but use chips (formulated to hold their shape during baking) as the add-ins.

Softened butter and all-purpose flour
  for the pan

6 ounces white chocolate, finely chopped

2¼ cups unbleached all-purpose flour

1/2 teaspoon salt

¼ teaspoon baking soda

¾ cup sugar

8 tablespoons (1 stick) salted butter,
  at room temperature

3 large eggs, at room temperature

½ cup buttermilk

Grated zest of 1 orange

¼ cup fresh orange juice

2 teaspoons pure vanilla extract

1 cup fresh or frozen whole cranberries
  (not thawed or chopped)

1 cup toasted, skinned, and coarsely
  chopped hazelnuts (see page 17)

1 cup (6 ounces) white chocolate chips

1. Position an oven rack in the center of the oven and preheat the oven to 350°F. Lightly butter and flour a 9-by-5-by-3-inch loaf pan and tap out the excess flour.

2. Put the chopped white chocolate in a heatproof bowl. Place in a skillet of barely simmer-ing water and let stand, stirring often, until melted and smooth; be sure not to get any water in the bowl. Remove from the water and let the chocolate cool until tepid.

3. In a medium bowl, whisk together the flour, salt, and baking soda. In a large bowl, beat the sugar and butter with an electric mixer set on high speed until light and fluffy, about 3 minutes. One at a time, beat in the eggs, beating well after each addition, and scraping down the sides of the bowl as needed. Beat in the buttermilk, followed by the tepid white chocolate, orange zest and juice, and vanilla. The mixture will look curdled, but don't worry. With the mixer on low speed, add the flour mixture, and beat just until smooth, scraping down the sides of the bowl as needed. Stir in the cranberries, hazelnuts, and white chocolate chips. Spread the batter in the prepared pan.

4. Bake until a bamboo skewer inserted in the center of the cake comes out clean, about 1½ hours. (This dense, moist cake has a longer baking time than other tea loaves.) Let cool on a wire cooling rack for 10 minutes. Invert the cake onto the wire rack and unmold. Turn right side up and let cool completely.

fruit and nut applesauce bread

Makes 10 servings

This wholesome loaf works equally well at breakfast or afternoon tea or as a simple evening dessert. The loaf gets extra flavor from Muscovado sugar, a deeply flavored brown sugar that is a by-product of traditional molasses production, but regular brown sugar can be substituted.

Softened butter and all-purpose flour for the pan

1 cup unbleached all-purpose flour

½ cup whole wheat flour

1½ teaspoons ground cinnamon

1 teaspoon baking soda

½ teaspoon salt

¼ teaspoon ground cloves

½ cup coarsely chopped walnuts

½ cup coarsely chopped pecans

½ cup dark raisins

½ cup golden raisins

½ cup pitted and chopped dates

8 tablespoons (1 stick) salted butter, at room temperature

½ cup firmly packed dark Muscovado sugar

1 large egg, at room temperature

1 teaspoon pure vanilla extract

1 cup applesauce

1. Position an oven rack in the center of the oven and preheat the oven to 350°F. Lightly butter and flour a 9-by-5-by-3-inch loaf pan and tap out the excess flour.

2. In a medium bowl, whisk together the all-purpose and whole wheat flours, cinnamon, baking soda, salt, and cloves. In another bowl, combine the walnuts, pecans, raisins, and dates. Add ¼ cup of the flour mixture and toss to coat the fruit and nuts.

3. In a large bowl, beat the butter with an electric mixer set on high speed until smooth, about 1 minute. Gradually add the Muscovado sugar and beat until light and fluffy, about 2 minutes. Beat in the egg, followed by the vanilla, and scrape down the sides of the bowl. Add the applesauce and mix well. With the mixer on low speed, gradually add the flour mixture, mixing just until combined, and scraping down the bowl as needed. Fold in the fruit and nut mixture, with its flour, making sure the flour is absorbed. Spread the batter in the prepared pan.

4. Bake until a bamboo skewer inserted into the center of the cake comes out clean, about 1 hour. Let cool in the pan on a wire cooling rack for 10 minutes. Invert the cake onto the rack and unmold, turn right side up and let cool completely.

sour cream coffee cake

Makes 12 to 16 servings

Although this was also included in Tate's Bake Shop Cookbook, *it such a classic that it bears repeating. It has an incredibly tender crumb and a ribbon of spiced pecans running through it. I like it warm, but it keeps well at room temperature and freezes perfectly.*

Softened butter and all-purpose flour
   for the pan

2 cups coarsely chopped pecans

2 cups sugar

1 tablespoon ground cinnamon

2¼ cups unbleached all-purpose flour

1 tablespoon baking powder

¼ teaspoon salt

½ pound (2 sticks) salted butter
   at room temperature

2 large eggs, at room temperature

1½ cups sour cream

1 tablespoon pure vanilla extract

1. Position an oven rack in the center of the oven and preheat the oven to 350°F. Lightly butter and flour a 10-inch fluted tube pan, and tap out the excess flour.

2. In a small bowl, combine the pecans, ½ cup of the sugar, and the cinnamon. In a medium bowl, whisk together the flour, baking powder, and salt. In a large bowl, beat the remaining 1½ cups sugar and the butter with an electric mixer set on high speed until light and fluffy, about 3 minutes. One at a time, beat in the eggs, beating well after each addition, and scraping down the sides of the bowl as needed. Beat in the sour cream and vanilla, scraping down the bowl as needed. With the mixer on low speed, add the flour mixture in thirds, beating just until smooth and scraping down the bowl as needed. Do not overmix.

3. Spread half of the batter in the prepared pan. Sprinkle in half of the pecan mixture. Top with the remaining batter and smooth the top. Sprinkle the remaining pecan mixture over the batter.

4. Bake until a long bamboo skewer inserted in the center of the cake comes out clean, about 1 hour. Let cool on a wire cooling rack for 10 minutes. Invert the cake and unmold onto the rack, and turn right side up. Let cool until warm or completely cool.

chocolate–blood orange marble cake

Makes 12 to 16 servings

My friend Jon Malkmes loves the combination of chocolate and orange, so I thought this would make him smile. The chocolate part is very rich, the orange is subtle, and the cake texture is very moist. Juice oranges can be substituted when blood oranges are not in season.

Cake

Softened butter and all-purpose flour
   for the pan

2 ounces unsweetened chocolate,
   coarsely chopped

2 ounces bittersweet chocolate,
   coarsely chopped

1¾ cups unbleached all-purpose flour

¾ teaspoon baking soda

¾ teaspoon baking powder

¼ teaspoon salt

½ pound (2 sticks) salted butter,
   at room temperature

1¼ cups sugar

3 large eggs, at room temperature

1 cup sour cream

1 tablespoon pure vanilla extract

½ cup miniature semisweet chocolate chips

Grated zest of 2 blood oranges

Syrup

½ cup fresh blood orange juice

¼ cup sugar

1. Position an oven rack in the center of the oven and preheat the oven to 350°F. Lightly butter and flour a 9-inch fluted or plain tube pan and tap out the excess flour.

2. To make the cake: In a microwave oven on Medium (50%) power, in a microwave-safe bowl, heat the unsweetened and bittersweet chocolates together for 30-second intervals, stirring after each interval, until melted, about 2 minutes. Let cool until tepid.

3. In a medium bowl, whisk together the flour, baking soda, baking powder, and salt. In a large bowl, beat the butter and sugar with an electric mixer set on high speed until light and fluffy, about 3 minutes. One at a time, beat in the eggs, scraping down the sides of the bowl after each addition. With the mixer on low speed, gradually add the flour mixture, and then the sour cream and vanilla.

4. Transfer half of the batter to a medium bowl. Add the tepid chocolate mixture and chocolate chips and stir well. Add the orange zest to the plain batter. Spoon the batters alternately into the prepared pan. Using a table knife, swirl them together to create a marbled effect.

(continued)

5. Bake until a long bamboo skewer inserted in the center of the cake comes out clean, about 50 minutes. Let cool in the pan on a wire cooling rack for 10 minutes.

6. Meanwhile, make the syrup: In a small saucepan, bring the orange juice and sugar to a boil over medium heat, stirring often to dissolve the sugar. Strain into a glass measuring cup.

7. Invert the cake onto the cooling rack and unmold. Place the rack on a plate. Slowly drizzle the orange syrup over the cake. Using a dessert spoon, retrieve the syrup on the plate and drizzle it back over the cake. Repeat until the cake absorbs all of the syrup. Let cool completely on the rack.

sweet potato cake

Makes 12 to 16 servings

This Bundt cake is a golden fall color, and a wonderful treat to serve with hot spiced cider after apple picking. It is important to start with baked sweet potatoes; leftovers work, but do not use canned yams. Savor its simplicity, or add pumpkin ice cream and caramel sauce to take it up a notch.

Pecan and Ginger Crumbs

1½ cups chopped pecans

¾ cup chopped crystallized ginger

¼ cup firmly packed dark brown sugar

2 tablespoons cold salted butter, cut into small pieces

Sweet Potato Cake

3 large sweet potatoes, scrubbed but unpeeled, each pricked a few times with a fork

Softened butter and all-purpose flour for the pan

3½ cups unbleached all-purpose flour

1 tablespoon baking powder

1 teaspoon ground cinnamon

½ teaspoon baking soda

½ teaspoon freshly grated nutmeg

½ teaspoon salt

½ pound (2 sticks) salted butter, at room temperature

1 cup firmly packed dark brown sugar

½ cup Grade B pure maple syrup

¼ cup granulated sugar

4 large eggs, at room temperature

1 tablespoon pure vanilla extract

½ cup sour cream

1. Position an oven rack in the center of the oven and preheat the oven to 400°F.

2. To make the crumbs: In a medium bowl, mix together the pecans, ginger, and brown sugar. Set aside.

3. To bake the sweet potatoes: Put the sweet potatoes on a rimmed baking sheet and bake until tender when pierced with the tip of a sharp knife, about 1 hour. Let cool until easy to handle. Peel and mash the sweet potato flesh in a bowl with a fork. You should have 2 cups mashed sweet potatoes. Let cool completely. Reduce the oven temperature to 325°F.

4. Lightly butter a 9-inch tube pan with a removable bottom (such as an angel food cake pan). Line the bottom of the pan with parchment or waxed paper. Dust the inside of the pan with flour and tap out the excess.

5. To make the cake: In a medium bowl, whisk together the flour, baking powder, cinnamon, baking soda, nutmeg, and salt. In a large bowl, beat the butter with an electric mixer set on high speed until creamy, about 1 minute. Gradually beat in the brown sugar, maple syrup, and granulated sugar, and beat until light and fluffy, about 2 minutes. One at a time, beat in the eggs, followed by the vanilla, scraping down the sides of the bowl as needed. Beat in half of the mashed sweet potatoes, mixing well; repeat. The mixture will look curdled, but don't worry. With the mixer on low speed, gradually add the flour mixture, then the sour cream, and mix just until smooth, scraping down the sides of the bowl as needed.

6. Spread half of the batter in the prepared pan, and sprinkle with 1¼ cups of the pecan crumbs. Top with the remaining batter and spread evenly. Add the 2 tablespoons cold butter to the remaining pecan crumbs, and, using your fingertips, work in the butter until the crumbs are moistened. Sprinkle over the top of the batter.

7. Bake until a long bamboo skewer inserted in the center of the cake comes out clean, about 1½ hours. Let cool on a wire cooling rack for 30 minutes. Run a dinner knife around the inside of the pan to release the cake. Lift up the insert. Invert the cake onto the wire rack and remove the insert and paper. Turn the cake right side up and let cool completely.

pumpkin apple cake

Makes 12 to 16 servings

This cake combines the best flavors of autumn. It is an effortless cake that is perfect for breakfast, a lunch box, or an afternoon snack. If serving to guests, dress up each serving with a spoonful of caramel sauce.

Softened butter and all-purpose flour for the pan

2 cups unbleached all-purpose flour

½ cup wheat germ

1 teaspoon baking powder

¾ teaspoon baking soda

½ teaspoon salt

½ teaspoon ground cinnamon

¼ teaspoon freshly grated nutmeg

¼ teaspoon ground cloves

¼ teaspoon ground ginger

8 tablespoons (1 stick) salted butter, at room temperature

¾ cup granulated sugar

½ cup firmly packed light or dark brown sugar

2 large eggs, at room temperature

1 teaspoon pure vanilla extract

1 cup solid-pack pumpkin (not pumpkin pie filling)

2 Granny Smith or Golden Delicious apples, peeled, cored, and cut into ½-inch dice (2 cups)

½ cup coarsely chopped walnuts

Confectioners' sugar for dusting

1. Position an oven rack in the center of the oven and preheat the oven to 350°F. Lightly butter and flour a 9-inch fluted or plain tube pan and tap out the excess flour.

2. In a medium bowl, whisk together the flour, wheat germ, baking powder, baking soda, salt, cinnamon, nutmeg, cloves, and ginger. In a large bowl, beat the butter with an electric mixer set on high speed until creamy, about 1 minute. Gradually beat in the granulated and brown sugars and beat until light and fluffy, about 2 minutes. One at a time, beat in the eggs, followed by the vanilla, scraping down the sides of the bowl as needed. Add the pumpkin and beat until combined. Add the apples and walnuts. With the mixer set on low speed, mix in the flour mixture in thirds, scraping down the sides of the bowl as needed. Spread the batter in the prepared pan.

3. Bake until the cake is golden brown and a long bamboo skewer inserted in the center of the cake comes out clean, about 1 hour. Let cool in the pan on a wire cooling rack for 15 minutes. Invert the cake onto the wire rack and unmold. Turn right side up and cool completely.

4. To serve, sift confectioners' sugar over the top and cut into wedges.

honey cake

Makes 2 loaves, 8 servings each

Not having honey cake in my heritage, I started from scratch to develop a recipe. I relied on my friend Sam Eber for a taste test. His reply? "It's the real thing, but better." Lighter honeys (such as orange blossom) tend to be milder in taste, while darker honeys (such as eucalyptus or buckwheat) have a more pronounced flavor.

Vegetable oil and all-purpose flour for the pan

3 cups unbleached all-purpose flour

¾ cup firmly packed dark brown sugar

½ cup granulated sugar

½ cup almond flour (or natural sliced almonds chopped very finely in a food processor)

1 tablespoon ground cinnamon

2 teaspoons baking powder

1½ teaspoons baking soda

½ teaspoon salt

¼ teaspoon ground allspice

¼ teaspoon freshly grated nutmeg

1 cup honey

1 cup cold brewed coffee

¾ cup vegetable oil

½ cup fresh orange juice

2 large eggs plus 1 large egg yolk, at room temperature

¼ cup applesauce

2 teaspoons pure vanilla extract

⅔ cup natural or blanched sliced almonds

1. Position an oven rack in the center of the oven and preheat the oven to 350°F. Lightly oil two 9-by-5-by-3-inch loaf pans. Line the bottoms of the pans with parchment or waxed paper. Dust the insides with flour and tap out the excess.

2. In a large bowl, whisk together the flour, brown sugar, granulated sugar, almond flour, cinnamon, baking powder, baking soda, salt, allspice, and nutmeg. Add the honey, coffee, oil, orange juice, eggs, yolk, applesauce, and vanilla and mix with an electric mixer set on low speed, just until smooth, scraping down the sides of the bowl as needed. The batter will seem thin. Divide the batter between the prepared pans. Top each with half of the sliced almonds. Place the pans on a large baking sheet.

3. Bake until a bamboo skewer inserted in the center of a loaf comes out clean, 50 to 60 minutes. Let cool in the pans on a wire cooling rack for 10 minutes. Invert the cakes onto the wire rack and unmold. Turn right side up and let cool completely. (The cake is fine the day of baking, but it gets even moister and more flavorful if wrapped in plastic wrap and stored at room temperature for a day or two.)

hakan's fresh fig cake

Makes 12 to 16 servings

*Monday through Friday, my friend Hakan Ciling designs for the textile and fashion indus-
tries. On the weekend, he is an equally talented baker, as this moist, fruit-studded cake shows.
If you are serving it for an evening dessert, top it with whipped cream flavored with ground
cinnamon or nutmeg.*

Softened butter and all-purpose flour
  for the pan

3 cups unbleached all-purpose flour

1 teaspoon baking soda

1 teaspoon salt

1¾ cups sugar

1¼ cups vegetable or grapeseed oil

3 large eggs, at room temperature

1 tablespoon pure vanilla extract

1 cup very coarsely chopped walnuts

1 cup dried cranberries

1 cup pitted dates or dried plums (prunes),
  cut in half

1 cup golden or dark raisins

12 ripe figs, tips trimmed and cut lengthwise
  into quarters (about 1½ cups)

1. Position an oven rack in the center of the oven and preheat the oven to 350°F. Lightly
butter and flour a 9-inch tube pan with a removable bottom (such as an angel food cake
pan) and tap out the excess flour.

2. In a medium bowl, whisk together the flour, baking soda, and salt. In a large bowl, beat
the sugar and oil with an electric mixer set on high speed until the mixture is very pale,
about 5 minutes. One at a time, beat in the eggs, followed by the vanilla, scraping down the
sides of the bowl as needed. With the mixer on low speed, gradually add the flour mixture
and mix just until combined, scraping down the bowl as needed. Fold in the walnuts, cranberries, dates, and raisins. The batter will be very thick.

3. Spread half of the batter in the prepared pan. Arrange half of the figs in a ring in the pan,
pressing them lightly into the batter. Repeat with the remaining batter and figs.

4. Bake until a long bamboo skewer inserted in the center of the cake comes out clean,
about 1¼ hours. Let cool in the pan on a wire cooling rack for 15 minutes. Run a knife
around the inside of the pan and the tube and lift out the insert. Invert the cake onto the
rack, unmold and let cool completely.

robin's blueberry buckle, julia's way!

Makes 6 to 8 servings

I came home one evening to find my two nieces, Julia and Kara, mixing up this delicious crumb-topped version of their mother Robin's blueberry buckle. Julia likes to serve it with a sour cream drizzle. The combination is scrumptious!

Cake

Softened butter and all-purpose flour for the pan

2 cups unbleached all-purpose flour

2 teaspoons baking powder

½ teaspoon salt

¾ cup sugar

4 tablespoons (½ stick) salted butter, at room temperature

½ cup milk

1 large egg, at room temperature

2 cups fresh or frozen blueberries (not thawed)

Topping

½ cup sugar

⅓ cup unbleached all-purpose flour

¼ cup rolled (old-fashioned) oats

4 tablespoons (½ stick) cold salted butter, cut into small pieces

½ teaspoon ground cinnamon

Drizzle

1 cup sour cream

2 tablespoons agave nectar or sugar, or to taste

¼ teaspoon pure vanilla extract

1. Position an oven rack in the center of the oven and preheat the oven to 350°F. Lightly butter and flour an 8-inch square baking pan and tap out the excess flour.

2. To make the cake: In a medium bowl, whisk together the flour, baking powder, and salt. In another medium bowl, beat the sugar and butter with an electric mixer set on high speed until light and fluffy, about 3 minutes. Add the milk and egg and beat until smooth, scraping down the sides of the bowl as needed. With the mixer on low speed, add the flour mixture, and mix just until smooth, scraping down the sides of the bowl as needed. Fold in the blueberries. Spread the batter in the prepared pan.

3. To make the topping: In a medium bowl, combine all of the ingredients, and, using your fingertips, work them together to make moist crumbs. Sprinkle evenly over the batter.

4. Bake until a wooden toothpick inserted in the center of the buckle comes out clean, about 55 minutes. Let cool completely in the pan on a wire cooling rack.

5. When ready to serve, make the sour cream drizzle: Whisk all of the ingredients together in a bowl, adding more nectar to taste if necessary. Cut the buckle into squares and serve on dessert plates, with the sour cream mixture drizzled on top.

Julia's Mini-Buckles: Julia likes to bake the batter in mini Bundt pans, and the little cakes do look cute as individual gifts! Butter and flour 4 mini Bundt pans and tap out the excess flour. Divide the batter among the pans and top with equal amounts of the crumb topping. Bake at 350°F until a wooden toothpick inserted in the center of a buckle comes out clean, 35 to 40 minutes. Invert the pans onto a large wire cooling rack and unmold the miniature buckles. Let cool completely on the rack.

pineapple toffee upside-down cake

Makes 8 servings

Looking for a way to increase the butterscotch flavor in old-fashioned pineapple upside-down cake, I used toffee bits in the topping. I left part of my test batch in my friend Nick Rutherford's mailbox. In less than an hour, I received this text: "OMG, this is the best pineapple upside-down cake I ever had, we already finished the entire thing!"

One 20-ounce can pineapple rings
   in juice or heavy syrup

12 tablespoons (1½ sticks) salted butter,
   4 tablespoons sliced, 8 tablespoons
   at room temperature

1 cup toffee bits

7 maraschino cherries,
   drained and stems removed

1½ cups unbleached all-purpose flour

1½ teaspoons baking powder

1 teaspoons baking soda

¼ teaspoon salt

¾ cup sugar

2 large eggs, at room temperature

1 teaspoon pure vanilla extract

¾ cup plain nonfat or low-fat Greek yogurt

1. Position an oven rack in the center of the oven and preheat the oven to 350°F.

2. Drain the pineapple, discarding the juice. Reserve 7 pineapple rings. Coarsely chop the remaining pineapple.

(continued)

3. Melt the 4 tablespoons of sliced butter in a 9-inch ovenproof skillet (see Note) over medium heat. Remove from the heat and sprinkle the toffee bits evenly into the skillet. Arrange the pineapple rings in the skillet, placing a cherry in the center of each one.

4. In a medium bowl, whisk together the flour, baking powder, baking soda, and salt. In a large bowl, beat the sugar and the 8 tablespoons room-temperature butter with an electric mixer set on high speed until light and fluffy, about 3 minutes. One at a time, beat in the eggs, followed by the vanilla, scraping down the sides of the bowl as needed. With the mixer on low speed, add the flour mixture in thirds, alternating with the yogurt in 2 equal additions, mixing just until smooth after each addition and scraping down the bowl as needed. Do not overmix. Stir in the chopped pineapple. Spread the batter evenly over the pineapple rings and cherries in the skillet.

5. Bake until the top is golden brown and a wooden toothpick inserted in the center of the cake comes out clean, about 40 minutes. Let cool in the pan for 5 minutes. Run a dinner knife around the inside of the skillet to loosen the cake. Place a serving plate over the skillet, and, using pot holders, invert the skillet and plate together to unmold the cake. (Return any pineapple rings that may be stuck to the skillet to their place on the cake.) Serve warm or at room temperature.

Note: You can bake the cake in 9-by-2-inch round cake pan instead of the skillet. Melt the butter and pour into the cake pan. The cake may take a few minutes longer to bake.

honeybell cake

Makes 12 servings

The Honeybell tangelo is considered the Queen of Oranges. Snowed in one afternoon, I created this cake to remind me that spring was on its way. By itself or with a cream cheese icing (such as the one on page 197), the cake is an orange-flavored treat, but the swirled orange-and-white topping makes it fit for an elegant dinner party. When you need something for a potluck, bring this, as it travels well and cuts easily; just keep the topping cold in a mini cooler.

Cake

Softened butter for the pan

2½ cups unbleached all-purpose flour

1 teaspoon baking powder

¾ teaspoon salt

½ teaspoon baking soda

1¾ cups sugar

10 tablespoons (1¼ sticks) salted butter, at room temperature

2 large eggs, at room temperature

¾ cup plain Greek yogurt

Grated zest of 1 tangelo, preferably Honeybell

½ cup fresh tangelo juice, preferably Honeybell

1 teaspoon pure vanilla extract

Topping

¼ cup plus 3 tablespoons sugar

2 large eggs plus 2 large egg yolk

½ cup fresh tangelo juice, preferably Honeybell

3 tablespoons fresh lemon juice

Pinch of salt

4 tablespoons (½ stick) cold unsalted butter, cut into tablespoons

Grated zest of 1 tangelo, preferably Honeybell

1 cup heavy cream

½ teaspoon orange extract or ¼ teaspoon orange oil

¼ cup plain Greek yogurt

1. Position an oven rack in the center of the oven and preheat the oven to 350°F. Lightly butter a 13-by-9-inch baking pan.

(continued)

2. To make the cake: In a medium bowl, whisk together the flour, baking powder, salt, and baking soda. In a large bowl, beat the sugar and butter together with an electric mixer set on high speed until light and fluffy, about 3 minutes. One at a time, beat in the eggs, scraping down the sides of a bowl as needed. Beat in the yogurt, tangelo zest, juice, and vanilla, scraping down the bowl. With the mixer on low speed, gradually mix in the flour mixture, scraping down the bowl as needed. Do not overmix. Spread the batter in the prepared pan.

3. Bake until a wooden toothpick inserted in the center of the cake comes out clean, about 40 minutes. Let cool completely in the pan on a wire cooling rack.

4. Meanwhile, to make the topping, first make a tangelo curd. In a heavy medium saucepan, whisk together ¼ cup of the sugar with the eggs and yolks. Whisk in the tangelo juice and lemon juice with the salt. Whisk constantly over medium-low heat until the mixture begins to thicken. Change to a heatproof spatula and stir constantly until the mixture is thick enough to coat the spatula, about 3 minutes total cooking time. (This will not be as thick as lemon curd; do not boil.) Remove from the heat heat and, 1 tablespoon at a time, whisk in the butter. Strain through a fine wire sieve into a small bowl to remove any bits of egg.

5. Stir the zest into the curd. Press plastic wrap directly against the curd surface. Refrigerate until chilled and thickened, at least 3 hours, or up to 12 hours.

6. Just before serving, in a medium bowl, whip the heavy cream, the remaining 3 tablespoons sugar, and the orange extract with an electric mixer set on high speed until the mixture forms soft peaks. Beat in the yogurt, until just combined. Fold in the curd, leaving some streaks of curd. Cut the cake and serve on dessert plates, topping each slice with a dollop of the topping.

chapter 3

pies, tarts, & crisps

TIPS FOR PIES AND TARTS

✳ Too much liquid can make pie dough soggy and too much flour makes a tough crust. Stir just enough liquid into the dry mixture to bring the dough together into clumps, then gather up the dough to make it cohere. Too much fat can make the pie dough crumbly, so don't add more thinking that it will make the dough tender.

✳ If pie (or cookie) dough has hardened in the refrigerator, let it stand at room temperature for 15 minutes to soften slightly before rolling.

✳ I prefer glass pie plates because they heat evenly and you can see how the crust is browning. I use two sizes of 9-inch pans: regular (about 1½ inches deep) and deep-dish (2 inches deep). Don't try to interchange them, as the difference is 2 cups of filling.

✳ Freeze unbaked pie shells in their pans, tightly wrapped in plastic wrap. Both crumb and pastry crusts can be baked from their frozen state.

✳ When making fruit desserts, use the best-tasting fruit possible. All of the sugar, butter, and spices in the world won't help a lackluster peach or mealy apple.

✳ For fruit pies, sprinkle cookie crumbs (graham cracker, sugar, or gingersnap) in the bottom of the pie shell. The crumbs soak up the filling juices and prevent the bottom crust from getting soggy.

✳ Tart dough needs to be supported in the pan so it stays in place during the initial baking. You can buy aluminum pastry weights or use uncooked dried beans. The beans can be saved for another use, but they will need to be replaced when they start to smell not-too-fresh.

three-berry crumb pie

Makes 8 servings

A member of Tate's Bake Shop's online Recipe of the Month Club requested this recipe. Serve it on the Fourth of July, with whipped cream as a red, white, and blue dessert.

All-purpose flour for rolling the dough

Buttermilk Pie Dough (page 96)
  or Lard Pie Dough (page 97)
  for a single-crust pie

2 tablespoons graham cracker crumbs

Crumb Topping

½ cup unbleached all-purpose flour

¼ cup very finely chopped almonds
  (use a blender or food processor)

⅓ cup sugar

4 tablespoons (½ stick) cold salted
  butter, cut into small pieces

Filling

2½ cups fresh strawberries, hulled and
  left whole if small, or cut in half if large

2 cups fresh blueberries

1½ cups fresh raspberries

¼ cup unbleached all-purpose flour

⅓ cup sugar

⅛ teaspoon ground cinnamon

1 tablespoon fresh lemon juice

1. Position a rack in the center of the oven and preheat the oven to 400°F. Line a large rimmed baking sheet with aluminum foil.

2. On a lightly floured work surface, roll out the pastry to fit a 9-by-2-inch deep-dish glass pie plate. Transfer to the pie plate and flute the edges. Sprinkle the graham cracker crumbs into the pie shell. Refrigerate while you make the filling.

3. To make the topping: In a medium bowl, mix together the flour, almonds, and sugar. Work in the butter with your fingertips until the mixture is moistened and crumbly. Refrigerate.

4. To make the filling: In a large bowl, mix together the strawberries, blueberries, and raspberries. In a small bowl, mix together the flour, sugar, and cinnamon. Sprinkle over the berries and toss gently until the berries are coated.

5. Spoon the berry mixture into the pie shell. Sprinkle the lemon juice on top. Sprinkle the crumb topping over the fruit, covering it. Put the pie on the baking sheet. Bake until the fruit is bubbling and the topping is golden brown, about 1 hour, 10 minutes. Let cool on a wire cooling rack. Serve warm or at room temperature. The pie is best served the day it is baked.

apple–italian plum deep-dish pie

Makes 8 servings

I first made this juicy and magnificent pie in mid-September when both fruits were in sea-
son. My friends Sam and Hakan could not wait to take the leftovers home. Note that this is a
deep-dish pie, so be sure to use a deep pie plate.

All-purpose flour for rolling the dough

Buttermilk Pie Dough (page 96)
  or Lard Pie Dough (page 97)
  for a double-crust pie

2 tablespoons crushed gingersnaps
  or graham crackers

4 peeled, cored, and sliced
  Granny Smith apples (4 cups)

1¾ pounds pitted and sliced
  Italian plums (4 cups)

½ cup firmly packed dark brown sugar

1 tablespoon unbleached all-purpose flour

1 teaspoon ground cinnamon

1 teaspoon ground ginger

2 tablespoons clear, golden, or dark rum

2 tablespoons cold salted butter,
  cut into small pieces

1. Position a rack in the center of the oven and preheat the oven to 400°F. Line a large rimmed baking sheet with aluminum foil.

2. On a lightly floured work surface, roll out 1 pastry disk to fit a 9-by-2-inch deep-dish glass pie plate. Transfer to the pie plate. Sprinkle the cookie crumbs evenly in the bottom of the crust. Refrigerate while you make the filling.

3. In a large bowl, toss together the apples, plums, brown sugar, flour, cinnamon, and ginger to coat the fruit. Sprinkle with the rum and toss again. Spoon into the pie shell and top with the butter pieces. Roll out the second pastry disk into a 10-inch round and center it over the fruit. Seal the edges of the dough and crimp as desired. Cut four 1-inch slits, almost connecting, in the center of the top crust. Place the pie on the baking sheet to catch the drippings.

4. Bake until the crust is golden brown and the fruit is bubbling and tender, about 1½ hours. If the crust starts to get too brown, lay a piece of aluminum foil loosely on top. Let cool completely on a wire cooling rack.

raspberry rhubarb pie

Makes 8 servings

Because rhubarb and raspberries aren't traditionally in season at the same time, you may have to use a frozen version of one or the other, but that will not affect the quality of this lovely, not-too-heavy dessert.

All-purpose flour for rolling the dough

Buttermilk Pie Dough (page 96)
  for a double-crust pie

2 tablespoons graham cracker crumbs
  or gingersnap crumbs

Filling

3 cups fresh or IQF (individually quick
  frozen, but not thawed) raspberries

3 cups (¼-inch thick) sliced fresh
  or frozen (not thawed) rhubarb

1 cup sugar

¼ cup unbleached all-purpose flour

2 tablespoons heavy cream

1 tablespoon fresh lemon juice

½ teaspoon pure vanilla extract

1 tablespoon cold salted butter,
  cut into small pieces

1. Preheat the oven to 400°F. Line a rimmed baking sheet with aluminum foil.

2. On a lightly floured work surface, roll out 1 pastry disk to fit a 9-by-2-inch deep-dish glass pie plate. Transfer to the pie plate. Sprinkle the cookie crumbs evenly in the bottom of the crust. Refrigerate the pie shell while you make the filling.

3. To make the filling: In a large bowl, toss together the raspberries, rhubarb, sugar, flour, cream, lemon juice, and vanilla until the fruit is evenly coated. Spoon into the pie shell and top with the butter pieces. Roll out the second pastry disk into a 10-inch round. Center it over the fruit. Seal the edges of the dough and flute as desired. Cut four 1-inch slits, almost connecting, in the center of the top crust. Place the pie on the baking sheet to catch the drippings.

4. Bake until the crust is golden brown and the fruit is bubbling and tender, about 1½ hours. (If using frozen fruit, the pie will take slightly longer to bake.) Let cool completely on a wire cooling rack.

brownie pie

Makes 8 to 10 servings

This flourless, gluten-free brownie pie makes a perfect dessert as is, or a base for ice cream and fudge sauce. You could also dress it up with whipped cream and raspberry sauce. If you add nuts, make sure they are finely chopped, because too-large nuts are unpleasant to eat in this soft, yummy chocolate dessert.

Pie

Softened butter for the pan

12 ounces semisweet chocolate, finely chopped

8 tablespoons (1 stick) salted butter, at room temperature

1 teaspoon pure vanilla extract

5 large eggs plus 4 large egg yolks, at room temperature

⅓ cup firmly packed dark brown sugar

½ cup Nutella or other chocolate-hazelnut spread, for serving

Nutella Whipped Cream (page 201) for serving

1. Preheat the oven to 325°F. Lightly butter a 9-inch glass pie plate.

2. To make the pie: In a microwave oven on Medium (50%), in a microwave-safe bowl, heat the chocolate and butter together, stirring occasionally, until just melted, about 2 minutes. Stir in the vanilla.

3. In a large bowl, beat the eggs and yolks together with an electric mixer set on high speed, until thickened and light in color, about 3 minutes. Add brown sugar and beat until light and fluffy. Add the chocolate mixture and mix until combined. Pour into the prepared pie plate.

4. Bake until a wooden toothpick inserted in the center of the pie comes out with moist, but not runny, crumbs, about 45 minutes. (In other words, bake it like a brownie.) Transfer to a wire cooling rack and let cool until warm or at room temperature.

5. Cut the pie into wedges and serve with a spoonful of the Nutella and a dollop of the whipped cream.

chocolate lime pie

Makes 8 servings

A Key lime pie, but lighter and quite a bit more interesting, can be served refrigerated or frozen. The ginger bits in the crust offer a nice, hidden surprise and the chocolate crust goes better with the lime filling than you might think! It's quick and easy and, unlike traditional Key lime pie, has no raw eggs to worry about. Serve the pie as it is, or top with whipped cream and a drizzle of raspberry coulis.

One 8-ounce package cream cheese, softened

¾ cup confectioners' sugar

Grated zest of 1 lime

One 14-ounce can sweetened condensed milk

½ cup fresh lime juice, preferably from Key limes

¾ cup heavy cream

Chocolate Ginger Crumb Crust (page 101)

1. In a large bowl, beat the cream cheese and confectioners' sugar with an electric mixer on medium speed until smooth. Mix in the lime zest. With the mixer running, pour in the condensed milk and lime juice, mixing until smooth, scraping down the sides of the bowl as needed.

2. In a medium bowl, whip the heavy cream until it forms soft peaks. Fold the whipped cream into the lime mixture. Pour into the prepared crust. Refrigerate until the filling is thoroughly chilled, at least 4 hours or up to 1 day. Serve chilled.

Frozen Chocolate Lime Pie: This is very refreshing in the summer. Wrap the pie well in plastic wrap and freeze until very firm, at least 4 hours, or up to 1 month. Thaw at room temperature for 30 minutes before serving.

chocolate pecan pie

Makes 8 servings

One of Tate's Bake Shop Facebook fans asked for this pie. I never thought I'd like it, fearing that it would be too sweet and rich for my taste, but the request made me try it once and for all. Not only did I love it, so did friends who had originally felt the same way I did. I simplified the recipe to just one pot, as the holidays can be so hectic. Thanks for the request, Laurie: this one's for you.

All-purpose flour for rolling the dough

Buttermilk Pie Dough (page 96) for a single-crust pie

½ cup firmly packed dark brown sugar

1 cup light corn syrup

8 tablespoons (1 stick) salted butter, at room temperature

1 tablespoon unbleached all-purpose flour

1 cup coarsely chopped pecans

½ cup semisweet chocolate chunks (see Note)

3 large eggs

1 teaspoon pure vanilla extract

1. On a lightly floured work surface, roll out the dough to fit a 9-inch pie plate. Transfer to the plate and partially bake according to the directions on page 95. Transfer to a wire cooling rack to cool.

2. Meanwhile, in a medium saucepan, bring the brown sugar and corn syrup to a boil over medium heat, stirring often. Remove from the heat. Add the butter, and stir until melted and smooth. Whisk in the flour. Let cool completely. (If the mixture is warm, it will melt the chocolate chunks.)

3. Position an oven rack in the center of the oven and preheat the oven to 350°F.

4. Put the cooled pie shell on a rimmed baking sheet. Sprinkle the pecans and chocolate chunks into the pie shell. Add the eggs and vanilla to the sugar mixture and whisk until combined. Pour over the pecans and chocolate.

5. Bake until the filling is completely puffed, about 45 minutes. Let cool completely on a wire cooling rack.

Note: If you don't want to buy chocolate chunks, chop a 3½-ounce semisweet chocolate bar into ½-inch pieces.

s'mores pie

Makes 8 servings

I have seen this pie make both adults and children smile. It is a combination of a chocolate cream pie and s'mores—a crispy graham cracker crust, with a creamy chocolaty pudding filling and a marshmallow meringue topping. For planning ahead, you can make and freeze the crust. Spread the pudding in the pie shell the night before serving, and refrigerate, then add the topping the next day.

Chocolate Pudding Filling

2 large eggs plus 1 large egg yolk

½ cup sugar

3 tablespoons cornstarch

2 cups milk

1 cup heavy cream

5 ounces milk chocolate, finely chopped

5 ounces semisweet chocolate, finely chopped

2 tablespoons salted butter, thinly sliced

2 teaspoons pure vanilla extract

Graham Cracker Crust (page 100), baked and cooled

Topping

¼ cup water

One ¼-ounce envelope unflavored gelatin

½ cup sugar

⅓ cup light corn syrup

Pinch of salt

4 large egg whites, at room temperature

2 teaspoons pure vanilla extract

1. To make the pudding filling: In a heatproof medium bowl, whisk together the eggs and yolk. Set aside. In the top of a double boiler, whisk the sugar and cornstarch well to combine. Gradually whisk in the milk and heavy cream. Cook over simmering water, stirring constantly, until the mixture begins to thicken, about 5 minutes. Add the milk and semisweet chocolates and stir until melted.

2. Whisk about one-third of the chocolate mixture into the egg mixture. Whisk back into the chocolate mixture and return to the double boiler. Continue stirring until the mixture thickens and just comes to a simmer, about 3 minutes. Remove from the heat and stir in the butter and vanilla. Strain the mixture through a wire sieve into a bowl to remove any bits of egg. Spread in the prepared crust. Cover with plastic wrap and refrigerate until chilled and set, at least 3 hours, or up to 1 day. (If you love "pudding skin," leave the filling uncovered.)

3. To make the topping: Pour the water into a ramekin or custard cup. Sprinkle in the gelatin and let stand until the gelatin softens, about 5 minutes.

4. In a small saucepan, stir together the dissolved gelatin, sugar, corn syrup, and salt. Attach a candy thermometer to the pan. Bring to a boil, stirring until the sugar dissolves, then stop stirring and boil until the mixture reaches 240°F. Reduce the heat to very low.

5. In the bowl of a standing heavy-duty mixer fitted with the whisk attachment, beat the whites on high speed until frothy. With the mixer running, drizzle in the hot syrup, avoiding the moving whisk, and beat until the mixture is cool, thick, and pure white, about 10 minutes. Beat in the vanilla.

6. Spoon the topping onto the pudding, piling it high in the middle, then spread it out to cover the entire top, making attractive peaks and swirls.

7. Position a broiler rack about 8 inches from the source of heat and preheat the broiler. Broil the pie, watching carefully, until the topping is lightly browned, which could be less than a minute. (If you have a culinary butane or propane torch, you can use that.) You don't want the whole top to be brown, just the peaks.

8. Using a sharp knife dipped into hot water between slices, cut the pie into wedges, and serve.

coconut custard pie

Makes 8 servings

Over the years, I was often asked to include coconut custard pie in our Thanksgiving offerings at Tate's Bake Shop. I finally created this recipe and now it is a great addition to the Bake Shop's holiday menu, as well as my family's table. The secret is big flakes of coconut or coconut chips, as opposed to the regular sweetened flakes.

All-purpose flour for rolling the dough

Buttermilk Pie Dough (page 96)
  or Lard Pie Dough (page 97)
  for a single-crust pie

1½ cups heavy cream

1 cup milk

3 large eggs plus 1 large egg yolk
  (save the white), at room temperature

¾ cup sugar

1 tablespoon pure vanilla extract

¼ teaspoon freshly grated nutmeg

¼ teaspoon salt

1 large egg white, beaten until foamy

1 cup unsweetened coconut chips (see Note)

1. Position an oven rack in the center of the oven and preheat the oven to 400°F.

2. On a lightly floured work surface, roll out the pie dough to fit a 9-inch pie plate. Transfer to the plate, flute the edges, and partially bake according to the directions on page 95. Transfer to a wire cooling rack and let cool while you make the filling.

3. In a small saucepan, heat the cream and milk just to a simmer. Remove from the heat. In a large bowl, whisk together the eggs, yolk, sugar, vanilla, nutmeg, and salt. Gradually whisk in the hot cream mixture.

4. Lightly brush the pie shell with some of the beaten egg white. Sprinkle the coconut chips evenly in the pie shell. Pour in the egg mixture.

5. Bake for 15 minutes. Reduce the oven temperature to 300°F and bake until the top is beginning to brown and the custard is jiggly but not liquid when shaken, about 35 minutes. Let the pie cool completely on a wire cooling rack. Refrigerate until chilled, at least 2 hours.

6. Cut the pie into wedges and serve chilled. (The pie is best eaten the day of baking, but it is fine the next day, too.)

Note: Coconut chips, large unsweetened coconut flakes, are available at natural food stores and online at www.superiornutstore.com. Regular flaked sweet coconut is also fine, but the results will be more along the lines of a traditional coconut pie.

meyer lemon mousse pie

Makes 8 servings

This pie is simple, light, and refreshing with the floral flavor of Meyer lemons. This citrus is a cross between an orange and a lemon and is in season in winter and early spring. Squeeze the juice when you find fresh ones and freeze for later use, or substitute a mix of regular lemon and orange juices. Serve this pie as is or with whipped cream flavored with lemon zest. It is perfect for a spring luncheon or after a summer seafood dinner.

Lemon Mousse

6 large egg yolks

¾ cup plus 2 tablespoons sugar

Grated zest of 1 Meyer lemon
or regular lemon

½ cup fresh Meyer lemon juice
or ¼ cup each fresh regular lemon
juice and orange juice

4 tablespoons (½ stick) salted butter,
cut into pieces, at room temperature

3 ounces white chocolate, finely chopped

1½ cups heavy cream

Sugar Cookie Crust (page 100),
baked and cooled

1. To make the mousse: In a medium saucepan, whisk together the egg yolks and ¾ cup of the sugar. Gradually whisk in the lemon zest and juice. Add the butter and whisk constantly over medium-low heat until the mixture is slightly thickened, about 3 minutes. It should be steaming, but do not let it boil, or it will curdle. Strain the mixture through a wire mesh sieve set over a bowl to remove any bits of egg. Add the white chocolate and whisk until melted and smooth. Let cool slightly.

2. Cover the lemon mixture with plastic wrap and refrigerate until chilled and beginning set, at least 2 hours, or up to 1 day.

3. To finish the mousse: whip the heavy cream and the remaining 2 tablespoons sugar with an electric mixer on high speed just until soft peaks form. Fold the whipped cream into the cold lemon mixture. Spread evenly into the prepared crust. Cover with plastic wrap and refrigerate again until chilled and set, at least 2 hours, or overnight.

4. Cut into wedges and serve chilled.

sour cream lemon pudding pie

Makes 8 servings

My son, Justin, was coming home for the Easter holidays. Knowing that he loves lemon and poppy seeds, but not cake, I put this pie together, and it was a big hit with the whole family. No one even missed the chocolate bunnies and jelly beans! It's lemony and very creamy, and the contrast of the crisp crust is heavenly.

Filling

¼ cup cornstarch

1 cup milk

3 large egg yolks

¾ cup sugar

Grated zest of 1 lemon

½ cup fresh lemon juice

1 cup sour cream

4 tablespoons (½ stick) unsalted butter, at room temperature

Sugar Cookie Crust with Poppy Seeds (page 100), baked and cooled

Whipped Cream (page 200)

1. To make the filling, in a medium bowl, whisk together the cornstarch and ½ cup of the milk to dissolve the cornstarch. Whisk in the egg yolks until smooth.

2. In a medium saucepan, combine the sugar, the remaining ½ cup milk, and lemon zest and juice and cook over low heat, stirring constantly, until the sugar dissolves and the mixture starts to simmer. Gradually whisk into the egg yolk mixture. Pour back into the saucepan and cook over low heat, stirring constantly, until the mixture comes to a simmer. Let bubble for 1 minute. Remove the pan from the heat. Add the sour cream and butter and whisk them in. Strain the filling through a fine wire sieve into a bowl to remove any bits of egg.

3. Pour the filling into the prepared crust. Cover with plastic wrap pressed directly against the filling to prevent a skin from forming. Refrigerate until the filling is chilled, at least 2 hours, or up to 1 day.

4. Just before serving, spread the whipped cream over the filling. Cut into wedges and serve chilled.

cutie pie

Makes 8 servings

One day I stopped at my local market for a box of clementines for my husband. While driving home, I noticed the label on the side of the crate: "Cutie Pie." I knew then that I had to create a pie with the same name, and here it is!

1¼ cups fresh clementine juice

One ¼-ounce envelope unflavored gelatin

8 ounces mascarpone or cream cheese (soften the cream cheese to room temperature)

1 cup confectioners' sugar

Grated zest of 2 clementines

1½ teaspoon orange oil or ¾ teaspoon orange extract

1½ cups heavy cream

Sugar Cookie Crust with Ginger (page 100)

1. Pour ¼ cup of the clementine juice into a ramekin or custard cup and sprinkle the gelatin on top. Set aside to soften the gelatin, about 5 minutes.

2. Meanwhile, in a medium saucepan, bring the remaining 1 cup clementine juice to a boil over high heat and cook until reduced to ¾ cup. Remove from the heat, add the softened gelatin, and stir well until dissolved. Let cool until tepid.

3. In a large bowl, beat the mascarpone and confectioners' sugar with an electric mixer set on high speed until smooth. Gradually beat in the clementine juice mixture, then beat in the clementine zest and orange oil, scraping down the sides of the bowl as needed.

4. In a medium bowl, whip the heavy cream with the electric mixer set on high speed until soft peaks form. Fold into the clementine mixture. Spoon into the prepared crust. Cover loosely with plastic wrap and refrigerate until the filling is chilled and set, at least 2 hours, or up to 1 day.

5. Cut the pie into wedges and serve chilled.

two-recipe pumpkin pie

Makes one 9-inch pie (8 servings), plus enough filling for 15 Pumpkin Pie Scones

When I heard that my sister-in-law, Robin King, was using pumpkin filling to moisten her scone dough, I thought, "That is so cool." One day, I came home to a surprise in my mailbox: a beautiful pumpkin scone in a brown paper bag, with the handwritten recipe. My version includes a single recipe that does double-duty as a pie filling (below) and as the liquid in the Pumpkin Pie Scones on page 38, or can be used to fill another pie.

All-purpose flour for rolling the dough

Buttermilk Pie Dough (page 96)
   or Lard Pie Dough (page 97)
   for a single-crust pie

Filling

3 large eggs

¾ cup packed dark brown sugar

2 tablespoons Grade B pure maple syrup

2½ cups solid-pack pumpkin
   (not pumpkin pie filling; about 1½
   [15-ounce] cans)

1 tablespoon ground cinnamon

1½ teaspoons ground ginger

1 teaspoon pure vanilla extract

¼ teaspoon freshly grated nutmeg

¼ teaspoon ground cloves

½ teaspoon salt

1½ cups heavy cream

Maple Whipped Cream (page 200)
   for serving

1. Preheat the oven to 350°F. On a lightly floured work surface, roll out the pastry to fit a 9-inch pie plate. Transfer to the pie plate and flute the edges. Refrigerate.

2. To make the filling: In a large bowl, whisk the eggs. Add the brown sugar and maple syrup and whisk again. Add the pumpkin, cinnamon, ginger, vanilla, nutmeg, cloves, and salt and whisk again. Add the heavy cream and whisk just until combined. Do not over-mix or the mixture will puff too much during baking. Measure 2 cups of the filling into a bowl, cover with plastic wrap, and refrigerate to make the Pumpkin Pie Scones on page 38. (The filling can be refrigerated for up to 1 day. Or freeze in an airtight container for up to 1 month.) Pour the remaining filling into the pie shell.

3. Bake until a wooden toothpick inserted in the center of the filling comes out clean (don't use your finger, or it will leave a mark, as I found from experience), about 1 hour. Let cool completely on a wire cooling rack. Refrigerate until chilled, at least 2 hours, or up to 1 day.

4. Cut into wedges and serve chilled, with a dollop of the maple whipped cream.

pumpkin mousse pie

Makes 8 servings

A delicious change from the traditional custardy pumpkin pie, this is smooth, light, and creamy, with a crisp, spicy crust. I recently taught this at the Southampton Historical Museum, where we only had one large pot, so I found out that the recipe can be easily multiplied and made into several pies for gifts! For an added treat, drizzle each slice with pure maple syrup before serving.

Pumpkin Mousse

¼ cup apple cider

One ¼-ounce envelope
  unflavored gelatin

½ cup firmly packed dark brown sugar

¼ cup cornstarch

1 teaspoon ground cinnamon

¾ teaspoon ground ginger

¼ teaspoon freshly grated nutmeg

⅛ teaspoon salt

¾ cup heavy cream

2 large egg yolks

1¾ cups milk

1 cup solid-pack pumpkin
  (not pumpkin pie filling)

2 teaspoons pure vanilla extract

Gingersnap Cookie Crust (page 100),
  baked and cooled

Maple Whipped Cream (page 200)

Pecan halves for garnish

1. To make the mousse: Pour the cider into a ramekin or custard cup. Sprinkle in the gelatin. Set aside to soften the gelatin, about 5 minutes.

2. In a medium saucepan, whisk together the brown sugar, cornstarch, cinnamon, ginger, nutmeg, and salt, being sure that the cornstarch is incorporated into the sugar. Add ¼ cup of cream and whisk until smooth. Add the yolks and whisk again. Add the milk and whisk until mixture is fully blended. Cook over medium-low heat, whisking often and occasionally switching to a heatproof spatula to scrape the corners of the pot, until the mixture is bubbling, about 5 minutes. Reduce the heat to low and cook for 30 seconds. Remove from the heat, add the gelatin, and whisk until thoroughly dissolved. Whisk in the pumpkin and vanilla. Transfer to a medium bowl and let cool slightly.

(continued)

3. Press a sheet of plastic wrap directly on the surface of the pumpkin mixture and refrigerate, stirring occasionally, until cool and beginning to set, about 1½ hours. If the mixture is lumpy, strain and press through a wire sieve into another bowl.

4. In a small bowl (or directly in a 2-cup glass measuring cup), whip the remaining ½ cup cream with an electric mixer set on high speed just until it thickens and holds it shape, not until stiff. Fold into the pumpkin mixture. Spread the filling evenly in the prepared crust. Cover loosely with plastic wrap and refrigerate until the filling is chilled and set, at least 4 hours, or up to 1 day.

5. Just before serving, spread the maple whipped cream over the top of the pie. Garnish with the pecan halves. Cut into wedges and serve chilled.

rhubarb brown betty

Makes 6 servings

A brown Betty is usually made with apples, but when rhubarb comes into its short season, I can't resist putting it into anything I can think of. I pick some at my family's farm to make this quick dessert. The buttery brioche crumbs and the tart rhubarb with just enough sugar to heighten its flavor is truly a delectable treat. Try it for breakfast, cold, topped with plain yogurt, a drizzle of honey, and some toasted oats.

Topping
7 cups (1-inch) cubed brioche
  or other rich white bread
8 tablespoons (1 stick) salted
  butter, melted

Softened butter for the baking dish

Filling
6 cups (1-inch-thick) sliced rhubarb
1 cup sugar (use 1¼ cups
  if you like sweeter desserts)

¼ cup fresh orange juice
1 teaspoon ground cinnamon
½ teaspoon ground ginger
½ cup water

Whipped Cream (page 200), for serving
Chopped crystallized ginger for garnish

1. To make the topping, position a rack in the center of the oven and preheat the oven to 250°F. Spread the bread cubes on a large rimmed baking sheet. Bake, stirring occasionally, until the cubes are dried but not toasted, about 30 minutes. Transfer to a large bowl and drizzle with the butter. Stir until the cubes are evenly moistened, crushing to make large crumbs.

2. Increase the oven temperature to 375°F. Butter the bottom of an 8-inch square baking dish or a gratin dish with an 8-cup capacity. Line a rimmed baking sheet with aluminum foil.

3. To make the filling: In a large bowl, mix together the rhubarb, sugar, orange juice, cinnamon, and ginger. Spread one-third of the bread crumbs in the baking dish. Top with half of the rhubarb. Repeat, then finish with the remaining breadcrumbs. The pan will look overfilled, but don't worry—it will cook down quite a bit. If you don't fill it high enough, it still tastes delicious but the appearance is lacking. Drizzle the water over the top. Cover tightly with aluminum foil.

4. Put the baking dish on the baking sheet. Bake for 40 minutes. Remove the foil and continue baking until the filling is bubbling and the topping is browned, about 20 minutes more. Let cool until warm.

5. Serve the Betty in bowls, topped with the whipped cream and sprinkled with crystallized ginger.

ginger plum crisp

Makes 4 to 6 servings

Small and egg-shaped with purple skin and yellow flesh, Italian prune plums are a sweet treat for a snack and hold their shape beautifully when baked. You might serve this crisp for breakfast, topped with Greek yogurt.

Topping
½ cup whole wheat flour
¼ cup old-fashioned (rolled) oats
¼ cup firmly packed dark brown sugar
½ teaspoon ground cinnamon
4 tablespoons (½ stick) cold salted butter, cut into small pieces
½ cup chopped pecans

Filling
2½ pounds Italian prune plums, pitted and cut lengthwise into quarters (about 5 cups)
2 tablespoons heavy cream
½ teaspoon pure vanilla extract
¼ cup granulated sugar
2 tablespoons chopped crystallized ginger

Vanilla ice cream for serving

1. Position an oven rack in the center of the oven and preheat the oven to 375°F. Have ready an 8-inch square baking dish.

2. To make the topping: In a medium bowl, mix the whole wheat flour, oats, brown sugar, and cinnamon. Add the butter and work it in with your fingertips until the mixture is blended and crumbly. Work in the pecans. (Stored in a zip-tight plastic bag, the topping can be refrigerated for a few days or frozen for up to a month.)

3. To make the filling: In the baking dish, combine the plums, cream, and vanilla. Add the granulated sugar and ginger and mix to coat the plums evenly. Sprinkle with the topping.

4. Bake until the fruit is bubbling and the topping is browned, about 35 minutes. Let cool slightly and serve warm, or at room temperature, with a scoop of ice cream.

cranberry pear crisp with chocolate

Makes 4 servings

I made this when a couple of friends came over for an impromptu dinner. Especially in winter, I like to use what I have in the house because it's too cold go out more than once! I love that it just serves four, with no leftovers, and how each bite has a different flavor. Sometimes you get chocolate with cranberries, and sometimes just pear and crumb. Eating it is addictive—my dinner guest Jeffrey Silberstein kept picking at the crisp after he finished his first bowl!

⅔ cup fresh or frozen
(not thawed) cranberries

3 ripe Anjou pears, peeled,
cored, and diced (3 cups)

¼ cup granulated sugar

1 teaspoon pure vanilla extract

Topping
⅓ cup old-fashioned (rolled) oats

⅓ cup unbleached all-purpose flour

⅓ cup firmly packed dark brown sugar

¼ teaspoon ground cinnamon

4 tablespoons (½ stick) cold salted
butter, cut into ½-inch cubes

⅓ cup coarsely chopped walnuts

⅓ cup semisweet chocolate chips

Whipped Cream (page 200)
or vanilla ice cream for serving

1. Position an oven rack in the center of the oven and preheat the oven to 375°F.

2. To make the filling: In a medium bowl, combine the cranberries and pears. Add the granulated sugar and vanilla and toss to combine. Pour into a 7- to 8-inch square baking dish. (I use a 7-inch square ceramic dish.)

3. To make the topping: In the same bowl, combine the oats, flour, brown sugar, and cinnamon. Using a pastry blender or your fingertips, work in the butter until the mixture is blended and crumbly. Work in the walnuts and chocolate chips. Sprinkle evenly over the pear mixture.

4. Bake until the fruit mixture has started to bubble up and the topping is beginning to brown, about 45 minutes. (The crisp may take less time in a larger dish, as the filling will be thinner than in a smaller dish.) Let cool slightly, and serve with the whipped cream.

chocolate raspberry tart

Makes 8 to 10 servings

This tart is a beautiful, almost black, sleek-looking dessert. The filling is smooth and not too sweet, and it is the perfect finish for a more sophisticated occasion. Leave it plain, top it with fresh raspberries, or garnish each serving with whipped cream and raspberry coulis. Do not cover the filling when chilling the tart, as that would mar the beautifully smooth top.

1¼ cups heavy cream
8 ounces bittersweet (62% cacao) chocolate, finely chopped
½ cup seedless raspberry jam
Chocolate Pastry Tart Crust (page 99), baked and cooled

1. In a medium saucepan, bring the cream to a boil over medium heat. Remove from the heat. Add the chocolate and let stand for 3 minutes to soften. Whisk until melted and smooth. Whisk in the jam. Pour into the prepared tart crust.

2. Refrigerate, uncovered, until the filling is chilled and set, at least 2 hours, and up to 1 day.

3. Remove the sides of the pan, cut into wedges, and serve chilled.

Gluten-Free Chocolate Raspberry Tart: Substitute the Nut Crust (page 184) for the Chocolate Pastry Tart Crust. Do not bake the nut crust.

chocolate praline tart

Makes 8 servings

The praline flavor really comes through in this tart and reminds me of a truffle that was my grandma's favorite. It is a great make-ahead dessert, because it can be made in stages: Bake the crust a few days ahead and freeze, make the easy filling and refrigerate to set, then make the whipped cream and serve.

Filling
1½ cups heavy cream
½ cup praline paste (see Note)
4½ ounces milk chocolate, coarsely chopped
4½ ounces semisweet chocolate, coarsely chopped

Chocolate Hazelnut Crumb Tart Crust (page 101)

Praline Whipped Cream
1 cup heavy cream
⅓ cup praline paste (see Note)
1 teaspoon pure vanilla extract

1. To make the filling: In a medium saucepan, bring the cream to a boil over medium heat. Remove from the heat and whisk in the praline paste. Add the milk and semisweet chocolates and let stand for 3 minutes to soften. Whisk until melted and smooth.

2. Pour into the prepared crust. Cover with plastic wrap and refrigerate until chilled, at least 2 hours, or up to 1 day.

3. Meanwhile, make the praline whipped cream: In a medium saucepan, bring the cream to a boil over medium heat. Remove from the heat and whisk in the praline paste and vanilla. Pour into a heatproof medium bowl and refrigerate until thoroughly chilled, at least 2 hours or overnight.

4. Just before serving, whip the cream with an electric mixer set on high speed until soft peaks form. Remove the sides of the tart pan. Cut into wedges and serve chilled, with the praline whipped cream.

Note: Praline paste is available at specialty food stores, some natural food stores, and on-line at www.kingarthurflour.com.

fresh fig tart

Makes 6 to 8 servings

Fig season is very short, so I advise eating as many as possible when you can. I enjoy them in sweets and in savory dishes. This tart is very simple, and the figs are the star.

All-purpose flour for rolling the dough

Tart Pastry Dough (page 98)

½ cup crème fraîche or ¼ cup each sour cream and heavy cream

2 tablespoons firmly packed light brown sugar

1 large egg yolk

1 teaspoon pure vanilla extract

12 ripe figs, stemmed and cut in half lengthwise

Whipped Cream (page 200) or vanilla ice cream for serving

1. On a lightly floured work surface, roll out the dough to fit into a 9-inch tart pan. Transfer to the pan, letting the excess dough hang over the sides. Roll the rolling pin over the top of the pan to cut off the overhanging dough. Prick the dough all over with a fork. Refrigerate for 30 minutes.

2. Preheat the oven to 350°F. Line the tart shell with aluminum foil and fill with small dried beans. Bake until the exposed dough is looks dry and set, about 15 minutes. Lift out and remove the foil with the beans. Prick the shell again and continue baking until crisp, about 10 minutes more. Set on a wire cooling rack. Increase the oven temperature to 400°F.

3. In a small bowl, whisk together the crème fraîche, brown sugar, egg yolk, and vanilla. Pour into the tart shell. Arrange the fig halves cut side up in the tart shell in a random pattern. Don't get the crème fraîche mixture on top of them.

4. Bake until the filling is set and beginning to brown, about 30 minutes. Let the tart cool in the pan on a wire cooling rack for 15 minutes. Remove the sides from the pan. Serve warm or at room temperature with the whipped cream.

blackberry galette

Makes 4 to 6 servings

When all the local farm stands are stocked with big baskets of berries, I can't resist buying them. I love the way blackberries cook up and hold their shape, with their sweet/tart taste. And the blackberries against the yellow hue of the cornmeal in the crust make a beautiful presentation. Serve this the day it is made, with fresh whipped cream or ice cream—it is lovely on its own, too!

Dough

1 cup unbleached all-purpose flour,
   plus more for rolling the dough

⅓ cup fine yellow cornmeal
   (not coarse cornmeal or polenta)

1 tablespoon sugar

¼ teaspoon salt

6 tablespoons (¾ stick) cold salted
   butter, cut into pieces

1 large egg yolk

2 tablespoons cold water

Filling

1 teaspoon unbleached all-purpose flour

2 cups fresh blackberries

3 tablespoons sugar

1 tablespoon cold salted butter,
   cut into small pieces

1 tablespoon sugar for sprinkling (optional)

1. To make the dough: In a medium bowl, mix together the flour, cornmeal, sugar, and salt. Work in the butter with a pastry blender, 2 knives, or your fingertips until the mixture resembles coarse meal with some small pea-sized pieces of butter. In a small bowl, mix together the egg yolk and water. Add to the flour mixture and stir gently with a fork until the mixture is moist enough to hold together.

2. Gather the dough into a thick disk. Wrap in plastic wrap and refrigerate until chilled but not hard, at least 30 minutes, or up to 2 hours. (The dough can be refrigerated for up to 2 days, but let it stand for 15 minutes before rolling out. It can also be frozen for up to 1 month.) *(continued)*

3. Preheat the oven to 400°F. Line a large rimmed baking sheet with a silicone baking mat or parchment paper.

4. On a lightly floured work surface, roll out the dough out into a 10-inch round about ⅛ inch thick. Fold the dough in half, and then reopen on the prepared baking sheet. The dough cracks easily, but just press it back together if it does, and don't worry, as the look of this dessert is very rustic.

5. For the filling: Sprinkle the 1 teaspoon flour over the dough leaving a 2-inch border all around. Spread the berries over the floured section of the dough. Sprinkle them with the sugar and dot with the butter. Fold the uncovered dough up over fruit, pleating it as necessary. If the dough cracks, not to worry—just seal the tears. If you wish, brush the edges of the dough with a pastry brush dipped in water and sprinkle with the tablespoon of sugar.

6. Bake until the crust starts to brown a bit and the fruit bubbles, about 40 minutes. Let the galette cool on the baking sheet. Transfer the galette to a serving platter with a wide spatula or pick up the baking mat and slide it off onto the platter.

PREBAKING PIECRUST

There are times when a piecrust should be completely or partially baked before adding the filling. Here's how to do it with Buttermilk Pie Dough or Lard Pie Dough (page 96 or 97).

To line the pie plate: On a lightly floured work surface, roll out 1 pastry disk into a round 4 inches larger than the bottom of the pie plate you are using (or 5 inches for a deep-dish pie plate). Fit it into the pie plate. Fold under the excess dough at the rim of the pie plate. Flute the dough as desired. Refrigerate the pie shell for 15 to 30 minutes. Prick the bottom of the crust with a fork to vent it. Lay a piece of aluminum foil over the entire surface of the dough and press so it conforms to the pie plate. Fill the foil-lined shell with small dried beans. (These can be used over and over again, until they smell "off.") Position an oven rack in the center of the oven and preheat the oven to 400°F.

For a partially baked piecrust, bake until the edge of the exposed dough is set and barely beginning to brown, about 15 minutes. Remove the foil with the beans.

For a fully baked piecrust, prick the crust again after you remove the foil and beans to keep it from puffing. Continue baking until golden brown, about 10 minutes more.

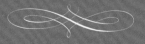

buttermilk pie dough

Makes enough for two 9- to 10-inch single-crust pies or one 9-inch double-crust pie

This is my go-to piecrust. You can use buttermilk or milk soured with vinegar (see page 15), and it makes an easy-to-handle dough that bakes into a tender, flaky crust. If you are just making a single-crust pie, freeze the remaining dough. You'll be glad you have it, ready to bake into a pie at another date.

2½ cups unbleached all-purpose flour

1 tablespoon sugar

¾ teaspoon salt

8 tablespoons (1 stick) cold salted butter, cut into ½-inch cubes

½ cup cold vegetable shortening, cut into ½-inch pieces

6 tablespoons cold buttermilk, or as needed

1. In a large bowl, combine the flour, sugar, and salt. Cut in the butter and shortening with a pastry blender or 2 knives until the mixture resembles coarse crumbs with a few pea-sized pieces of fat. (You can also use your fingertips, but work quickly or the fats will soften, and you want them to stay cold.) Stir in just enough buttermilk until the dough clumps together; you don't want it wet.

2. Press the dough together and divide it in half. Shape each half into a thick disk and wrap each one in plastic wrap. Refrigerate until chilled, about 1 hour. Pie dough is easier to roll out if it is chilled but not rock hard. (The dough can be frozen, wrapped in plastic wrap and stored in a zip-tight bag, for up to 1 month. Thaw in the refrigerator overnight.)

lard pie dough

Makes enough for two 9-inch single-crust pies or one 9-inch double-crust pie

This is my favorite pie dough to for my home baking—as long as I don't have vegetarians coming for dinner. Lard pie crust yields the flakiest, crispest crust you will ever make. I use a combination of lard and butter to get the flavor of butter with the tenderizing qualities of lard. Look for rendered leaf lard at your farmers' market, or purchase it online, as I do, from D'Angelo Brothers in Philadelphia, at www.dangelobros.com. Cut it into pieces and freeze in a zip-tight plastic bag, ready to go for your pastry making. Supermarket lard works fine, but it isn't as fresh and natural as the butcher product.

1½ cups unbleached all-purpose flour

¾ cup unbleached cake flour (see Note)

2 tablespoons sugar

½ teaspoon salt

⅛ teaspoon baking powder

12 tablespoons (1½ sticks) cold salted butter, cut into ½-inch cubes

6 tablespoons cold leaf lard, cut into ½-inch cubes

½ cup buttermilk, or as needed

1. In a large bowl, combine the all-purpose flour, cake flour, sugar, salt, and baking powder. Cut in the butter and shortening with a pastry blender or 2 knives until the mixture resembles coarse crumbs with a few pea-sized pieces of fat. (You can use your fingertips, but work quickly, or the fats will soften, and you want them to stay cold.) Stir in just enough buttermilk until the dough clumps together; you don't want it wet.

2. Press the dough together and divide it in half. Shape each into a thick disk and wrap each one in plastic wrap. Refrigerate until chilled, about 1 hour. Pie dough is easier to roll out if it is chilled but not rock hard. (The dough can be frozen, wrapped in plastic wrap and stored in a zip-tight bag, for up to 1 month. Thaw in the refrigerator overnight.)

Note: Unbleached cake flour can be purchased at many specialty food stores and online from www.kingarthurflour.com. If you must use bleached cake flour, be sure it isn't self-rising flour.

tart pastry dough

Makes enough for one 9-inch tart shell

This crisp and buttery pastry has been in my life for many years. When I was attending a pastry class, a fellow student gave me her fail-proof tart dough recipe, and she was right— it is a great one.

1½ cups unbleached all-purpose flour

2 tablespoons sugar

¼ teaspoon salt

8 tablespoons (1 stick) cold salted butter, cut into ½-inch cubes

2 tablespoons heavy cream

1 large egg yolk

1. In a large bowl, combine the flour, sugar, and salt. Work in the butter with a pastry blender or 2 knives (or your fingertips) until the mixture resembles coarse crumbs with a few pea-sized pieces of butter. In a ramekin, mix together the heavy cream and egg yolk. Drizzle over the flour mixture and stir until the dough clumps together. Gather up the dough and shape into a thick disk.

2. Wrap the dough in plastic wrap and refrigerate until chilled, at least 1 hour, or up to 1 day. (The dough is easiest to roll out if chilled but not rock hard. If it is very cold and firm, let stand at room temperature for about 15 minutes before rolling.)

chocolate pastry tart crust

Makes one 9-inch tart shell

This tart crust can be used for any of your favorite tarts. It's very dark but light and crisp. Use it with the chocolate raspberry tart or fill with ice cream and chocolate sauce; even a banana cream tart would be amazing!

10 tablespoons (1¼ sticks) salted butter, at room temperature

½ cup firmly packed dark brown sugar

1 teaspoon pure vanilla extract

6 tablespoons Dutch-processed cocoa powder,
   plus more for rolling the dough

1 cup unbleached all-purpose flour

1. In a large bowl, beat the butter, brown sugar, and vanilla with an electric hand mixer set on high speed until light and fluffy, about 2 minutes. With the mixer on low speed, beat in the cocoa powder. With the mixer on low speed, add the flour and mix until combined. Shape into a thick disk and wrap in plastic wrap. Refrigerate until chilled, at least 2 hours, or up to 1 day. (The dough is easiest to roll out if chilled but not rock hard. If it is very cold and firm, let stand at room temperature for about 15 minutes before rolling.)

2. Dust a work surface with cocoa powder. (Flour leaves marks on the dark cocoa dough that I don't like.) Roll the dough out into a 12-inch round about ⅛ inch thick. Transfer to a 9-inch tart pan with a removable bottom. Roll a rolling pin over the top of the pan to cut off the excess dough. Freeze for at least 30 minutes. (Or cover with plastic wrap and freeze for up to 1 month. Thaw in the refrigerator before using.)

3. Position an oven rack in the center of the oven and preheat the oven to 375°F.

4. Put the tart pan on a rimmed baking sheet. Prick the bottom of the crust with a fork to vent it. Lay a piece of aluminum foil over the entire surface of the dough and press so it conforms to the tart pan. Fill the foil-lined shell with small dried beans. Bake until the exposed dough looks set, about 20 minutes. Lift off the foil with the beans. Continue baking, pricking the crust again if it puffs, until the pastry looks crisp, about 10 minutes more. Let cool completely on a wire cooling rack.

sugar cookie crust

Makes one 9-inch pie or tart crust

When you aren't up for making pastry, delicious and simple cookie crusts come to the rescue. Here is a basic crust made with Tate's Sugar Cookies (yes, you can use another brand), as well as several variations for a variety of fillings. Use a food processor to crush the cookies into crumbs. Or put them in a zip-tight plastic bag and crush them with a rolling pin.

  2 cups finely crushed sugar cookies, preferably Tate's
  (about one 8-ounce package)
  3 tablespoons salted butter, melted

1. Position an oven rack in the center of the oven and preheat the oven to 350°F.

2. Pulse the cookie crumbs and melted butter in a food processor until combined. Pour the crumb mixture into a 9-inch pie plate or tart pan with a removable bottom and press the mixture evenly against the bottom and sides of the pan. Make sure that the crust is not too thick in the corners. Do not press too firmly, or the crust will be hard.

3. Put the pan on a baking sheet. Bake until the crust smells sweet and toasty, about 10 minutes. Let cool completely on a wire cooling rack.

Gingersnap Cookie Crust: Substitute finely crushed gingersnaps for the sugar cookies, add 1 tablespoon dark brown sugar, and pulse until combined. Add 6 tablespoons (¾ stick) salted butter, melted, and pulse until moistened.

Graham Cracker Crust: Substitute finely crushed graham crackers for the sugar cookies, add 1 tablespoon granulated sugar, and pulse until combined. Add 6 tablespoons (¾ stick) salted butter, melted, and pulse until moistened.

Sugar Cookie Crust with Ginger: Add ¼ cup finely chopped crystallized ginger to the cookie crumbs and pulse just to combine before adding the melted butter.

Sugar Cookie Crust with Poppy Seeds: Add 2 tablespoons poppy seeds to the cookie crumbs and pulse just to combine before adding the melted butter.

chocolate cookie crumb crust

Makes one 9-inch piecrust

This no-bake crumb crust can be used for ice cream pie, chocolate cream pie, or cheesecake, among other desserts. I give a couple of variations. The ginger version goes surprisingly well with many flavors, but it's all about taste and what you like.

2 cups chocolate wafer cookie crumbs
6 tablespoons (¾ stick) unsalted butter, melted

1. In a medium bowl, using a spoon or your hands, mix the cookie crumbs and melted butter. (I actually mix it right in the pie plate to save clean-up.)

2. Pour the crumb mixture into a 9-inch pie plate and press it evenly against the bottom and the sides of pan. Refrigerate while you make the filling, or wrap tightly in plastic wrap and freeze for up to 1 month.

Chocolate Ginger Crumb Crust: Substitute ½ cup finely chopped crystallized ginger for an equal amount of the chocolate wafer cookie crumbs.

Chocolate Hazelnut Crumb Tart Crust: This is especially good with a chocolate mousse filling, or use your favorite pudding or ice cream. Pulse ⅓ cup toasted and skinned hazelnuts (see page 17) in a food processor until finely chopped. Add 1 cup chocolate wafer cookie crumbs, 4 tablespoons (½ stick) unsalted butter, melted, and 2 tablespoons light brown sugar and pulse to combine. Press into a 9-inch tart pan with a removable bottom.

chapter 4

cookies

TIPS FOR COOKIES

✳ Always let baking sheets cool between batches. If the dough is placed on warm sheets, it could start to melt before it goes into the oven, resulting in flat cookies. Especially during holiday baking season, have extra baking sheets so you can bake batch after batch without waiting. Don't rinse hot baking sheets under cold water to cool them, or they may warp.

✳ For lining baking sheets, use no-hassle parchment paper. To get rolled paper to lay flat in the sheet, put a dab of butter in the corners of the baking sheet to hold the paper in place. I also love silicone baking mats (often sold under the brand name Silpat), which are reusable and sturdy. But you can always grease baking sheets the old-fashioned way, with butter, vegetable shortening, or nonstick vegetable oil spray.

✳ Many cookie recipes start by the creaming butter and sugar together. Most cookies aren't meant to be light and fluffy, so mix the butter and sugar only until combined and beginning to turn pale, about 1 minute.

✳ For even baking, drop cookies should be made with equal amounts of dough. A 1-ounce (2-tablespoon) food portion scoop does a wonderful job.

✳ If your cookies brown too quickly on the bottom, stack the sheet of cookies on a second baking sheet. This insulates the top sheet so the cookies bake at a slower rate.

✳ Cookies made with vegetable shortening will spread less than those made with butter. Shortening melts at a higher temperature than butter, so the cookies hold their shape longer.

✳ Bar cookies or brownies can be difficult to remove from the pan without breaking the first one. If you line the pan with aluminum foil before baking, the entire baked bar can be lifted out in one piece for easy cutting. Line the bottom and two opposite sides of the baking pan with a long piece of aluminum foil, allowing about 2 inches of excess foil at both ends. Pleat the foil down the center to fit as needed.

chocolate mint cookies

Makes 3 dozen cookies

When I was kid, I loved anything with the combination of mint and chocolate. Now that I'm an adult, the love affair continues. These soft and chewy cookies celebrate that pairing, so pour yourself a big glass of milk and feel free to dunk.

2 cups unbleached all-purpose flour

½ cup natural cocoa powder

1 teaspoon baking soda

½ teaspoon salt

½ pound (2 sticks) salted butter, at room temperature

1 cup granulated sugar

¾ cup firmly packed dark brown sugar

2 large eggs, at room temperature

1 tablespoon peppermint extract

1 teaspoon pure vanilla extract

2 cups (12 ounces) semisweet chocolate chips

1. Position the oven racks in the top third and center of the oven and preheat the oven to 375°F. Line 2 large rimmed baking sheets with parchment paper or silicone baking mats.

2. In a medium bowl, whisk together the flour, cocoa powder, baking soda, and salt. In a large bowl, beat the butter, granulated sugar, and brown sugar with an electric mixer set on high speed until combined, about 1 minute. One at a time, beat in the eggs, followed by the peppermint extract and vanilla. With the mixer on low speed, mix in the flour mixture, just until combined. Mix in the chocolate chips.

3. Using 2 tablespoons per cookie, drop the dough 3 inches apart onto the prepared baking sheets. (Or use a 1-ounce food portion scoop to scoop the dough onto the baking sheets.) Refrigerate the remaining dough while you bake the first batch.

4. Bake, rotating the positions of the sheets from top to bottom and front to back halfway through baking, until the edges of the cookies are lightly browned, 8 to 10 minutes. Do not overbake. Let cool on the baking sheets for 5 minutes. Transfer to wire cooling racks and let cool completely. Repeat with the remaining dough, on cooled baking sheets.

peanut butter chocolate chip cookies

Makes 2½ dozen cookies

My Facebook fans Jim and Holly asked for advice on how to make a soft and chewy peanut butter cookie with chocolate, so I developed this recipe just for them. (Vegetable shortening or coconut oil, both of which are soft at room temperature, lend their texture to the cookies.) This is a sensational cookie, but if you want peanuts through and through, substitute peanut butter chips for the chocolate ones.

1½ cups unbleached all-purpose flour

1 teaspoon baking soda

¼ teaspoon salt

1 cup firmly packed dark brown sugar

4 tablespoons (½ stick) salted butter, at room temperature

¼ cup vegetable shortening or coconut oil

1 large egg plus 1 large egg yolk, at room temperature

½ teaspoon pure vanilla extract

1 cup smooth peanut butter

1½ cups (9 ounces) chocolate chips

1. Position the oven racks in the top third and center of the oven and preheat the oven to 325°F. Line 2 large rimmed baking sheets with parchment paper or silicone baking mats.

2. In a medium bowl, whisk together the flour, baking soda, and salt. In a large bowl, beat the brown sugar, butter, and shortening with an electric mixer set on high speed until combined, about 1 minute. Beat in the egg, followed by the egg yolk and vanilla. Add the peanut butter and mix well. With the mixer on low speed, mix in the flour mixture, just until combined. Mix in the chocolate chips.

3. Roll the dough into 30 walnut-sized balls. Arrange about 2 inches apart on the prepared baking sheets. Using a dinner fork, press an X into the top of each cookie, flattening it to about half of its original thickness. Refrigerate the remaining dough balls on a plate while you bake the first batch.

4. Bake, rotating the positions of the sheets from top to bottom and front to back halfway through baking, until the cookies are golden brown, about 20 minutes. Let cool on the baking sheets for 5 minutes. Transfer to a wire cooling rack and let cool completely. Repeat with the remaining dough balls, using cooled baking sheets.

candy cane chocolate chip cookies

Makes about 3½ dozen cookies

Here's what I do with the leftover and broken candy canes in the Bake Shop during Christmas season: turn them into these confection-like mint cookies. To crush the candy canes, leave them in their wrappers and lightly tap with the handle of a dinner knife or a hammer until they are pieces about the size of a miniature chocolate chip.

2 cups plus 2 tablespoons unbleached all-purpose flour

1 teaspoon baking soda

1 teaspoon salt

½ pound (2 sticks) salted butter, at room temperature

1 cup granulated sugar

½ cup firmly packed dark Muscovado (see page 48) or brown sugar

2 large eggs, at room temperature

1 teaspoon pure vanilla extract

1 teaspoon water

2 cups (12 ounces) semisweet chocolate chips

1 cup coarsely crushed candy canes

1. Position the oven racks in the top third and center of the oven and preheat the oven to 325°F. Line 2 large rimmed baking sheets with parchment paper or silicone baking mats.

2. In a medium bowl, whisk together the flour, baking soda, and salt. In a large bowl, beat the butter, granulated sugar, and brown sugar with an electric mixer set on high speed until combined, about 1 minute. One at a time, beat in the eggs, followed by the vanilla and water. With the mixer on low speed, mix in the flour mixture, just until combined. Mix in the chocolate chips and crushed candy canes.

3. Using 2 tablespoons per cookie, drop the dough 3 inches apart onto the prepared baking sheets. (Or use a 1-ounce food portion scoop to scoop the dough onto the baking sheets.)

4. Bake, rotating the positions of the sheets from top to bottom and front to back halfway through baking, until the cookies are golden brown, about 20 minutes. Let cool on the baking sheets for 5 minutes. Transfer to wire cooling racks and let cool completely. Repeat with the remaining dough, on cooled baking sheets.

chunkies

Makes about 3 dozen cookies

When I first published this recipe, it became my friend Rick Harrington's favorite cookie to bake for his kids. These cookies are full of flavor and texture and will remind you of a Nestlé Chunky candy bar.

1¼ cups unbleached all-purpose flour

½ teaspoon baking soda

½ teaspoon salt

8 tablespoons (1 stick) salted butter, at room temperature

½ cup firmly packed dark brown sugar

¼ cup granulated sugar

1 large egg, at room temperature

1 teaspoon pure vanilla extract

1 cup (6 ounces) semisweet chocolate chips

1 cup dark raisins

1 cup toasted and coarsely chopped walnuts

1. Position the oven racks in the top third and center of the oven and preheat the oven to 350°F. Line 2 large rimmed baking sheets with parchment paper or silicone baking mats.

2. In a small bowl, whisk together the flour, baking soda, and salt. In a large bowl, beat the butter, brown sugar, and granulated sugar with an electric mixer set on high speed until combined, about 1 minute. Beat in the egg and vanilla. With the mixer on low speed, mix in flour mixture, just until combined. Mix in the chocolate chips, raisins, and walnuts.

3. Using 2 tablespoons per cookie, drop the dough about 2 inches apart onto the prepared baking sheets. (Or use a 1-ounce food portion scoop to scoop the dough onto the baking sheets.)

4. Bake, rotating the positions of the sheets from top to bottom and front to back halfway through baking, until the cookies start to brown on the edges, about 12 minutes Let cool on the baking sheets for 5 minutes. Transfer to a wire cooling rack and let cool completely. Repeat with the remaining dough, on cooled baking sheets.

chubby tates

Makes about 3 dozen cookies

This one is for those of you that appreciate thick, soft, chewy chocolate chip cookies. I love to eat them warm, when the chips are still melted. See my instructions for freezing the dough—I am never without ready-to-bake frozen balls of "Chubbies" dough for a just-baked treat.

2¼ cups unbleached all-purpose flour

1 teaspoon baking soda

1 teaspoon salt

1 cup firmly packed dark brown sugar

12 tablespoons (1½ sticks) salted butter, at room temperature

½ cup granulated sugar

1 tablespoon light corn syrup

1 large egg plus 1 large egg yolk, at room temperature

2 teaspoons pure vanilla extract

2 cups (12 ounces) semisweet chocolate chips

1. Position the oven racks in the top third and center of the oven and preheat the oven to 325°F. Line 2 large rimmed baking sheets with parchment paper or silicone baking mats.

2. In a medium bowl, whisk together the flour, baking soda, and salt. In a large bowl, beat the brown sugar, butter, granulated sugar, and corn syrup with an electric mixer set on high speed until combined, about 1 minute. Beat in the egg, egg yolk, and vanilla. With the mixer on low speed, mix in the flour mixture, just until combined. Mix in the chocolate chips.

3. Using 2 tablespoons per cookie, drop the dough about 3 inches apart onto the prepared baking sheets. (Or use a 1-ounce food portion scoop to scoop the dough onto the baking sheets.) The mounds of dough can be frozen on the baking sheets until hard, then transferred to a zip-tight plastic bag and frozen for up to 1 month. Bake without thawing.

4. Bake, rotating the positions of the sheets from top to bottom and front to back halfway through baking, until the cookies are lightly browned on the edges, about 18 minutes. (If using frozen cookies, bake for about 20 minutes.) Let cool on the baking sheets for 5 minutes. Transfer to a wire cooling rack and let cool completely. Repeat with the remaining dough, on cool baking sheets.

macadamia chocolate chip cookies

Makes about 3½ dozen cookies

Playing one intensely flavored ingredient off another, these cookies are truly decadent. A lower oven temperature lets the cookies bake thin and crisp. For softer, thicker cookies, bake them at 350°F for 15 minutes. To crush the nuts, place them in a zip-tight bag and rap them with a rolling pin. This is much easier than trying to chop the round nuts with a knife.

1¾ cups unbleached all-purpose flour

1½ cups old-fashioned (rolled) oats

1 teaspoon baking soda

1 teaspoon salt

1¼ cups firmly packed dark brown sugar

½ pound (2 sticks) salted butter,
   at room temperature

½ cup granulated sugar

2 large eggs, at room temperature

1½ teaspoons pure vanilla extract

1½ cups (9 ounces) semisweet chocolate chips

1 cup coarsely crushed macadamia nuts

1. Position the oven racks in the top third and center of the oven and preheat the oven to 325°F. Line 2 large rimmed baking sheets with parchment paper or silicone baking mats.

2. In a medium bowl, whisk together the flour, oats, baking soda, and salt. In a large bowl, beat the brown sugar, butter, and granulated sugar with an electric mixer set on high speed until combined, about 1 minute. One at a time, beat in the eggs, followed by the vanilla. With the mixer on low speed, mix in the flour mixture, just until combined. Mix in the chocolate chips and macadamia nuts.

3. Using 2 tablespoons per cookie, drop the dough 3 inches apart onto the prepared baking sheets. (Or use a 1-ounce food portion scoop to scoop the dough onto the baking sheets.)

4. Bake, rotating the positions of the sheets from top to bottom and front to back halfway through baking, until the cookies are golden brown, about 25 minutes. Let cool on the baking sheets for 5 minutes. Transfer to a wire cooling rack and let cool completely. Repeat with the remaining dough, using cooled baking sheets.

pumpkin chocolate chip cookies

Makes 5 dozen cookies

Because chocolate chip cookies are my favorite cookies, I believe they should be enhanced to represent all the different seasons. This is my version for fall: spicy, soft, and cakey, with dark chocolate chips, chewy tart cranberries, and crunchy toasted pecans. When I offered samples at the Bake Shop, the customers bought up the whole batch, and that is always a good sign.

1½ cups unbleached all-purpose flour

½ cup old-fashioned (rolled) oats

2 teaspoons ground cinnamon

1 teaspoon baking soda

1 teaspoon ground ginger

¾ teaspoon salt

¼ teaspoon freshly grated nutmeg

¼ teaspoon baking powder

¼ teaspoon ground allspice
   or ground cloves (optional)

½ pound (2 sticks) salted butter,
   at room temperature

1 cup firmly packed dark brown sugar

½ cup granulated sugar

One 15-ounce can solid-pack pumpkin
   (not pumpkin pie filling)

2 large eggs, at room temperature

2 teaspoons pure vanilla extract

2 cups (12 ounces) semisweet chocolate chips

1 cup toasted and coarsely chopped pecans

1 cup dried cranberries

1. Position the oven racks in the top third and center of the oven and preheat the oven to 350°F. Line 2 large rimmed baking sheets with parchment paper or silicone baking mats.

2. In a medium bowl, whisk together the flour, oats, cinnamon, baking soda, ginger, salt, nutmeg, baking powder, and allspice, if using. In a large bowl, beat the butter, brown sugar, and granulated sugar with an electric mixer set on high speed until combined, about 1 minute. Beat in the pumpkin. One at a time, beat in the eggs, followed by the vanilla. With the mixer on low speed, mix in the flour mixture, just until combined. Stir in the chocolate chips, pecans, and cranberries.

3. Using 2 tablespoons per cookie, drop the dough 3 inches apart onto the prepared baking sheets. (Or use a 1-ounce food portion scoop to scoop the dough onto the baking sheets.) Bake, rotating the positions of the sheets from top to bottom and front to back halfway through baking, until a cookie springs back when pressed in the center, about 15 minutes. Let cool on the baking sheets for 5 minutes. Transfer to a wire cooling rack and let cool completely. Repeat with the remaining dough, using cooled baking sheets.

cowboy cookies

Makes about 4 dozen cookies

An old family friend, Sharon Nasti, gave me this recipe many years ago. It is a rib-sticking, hearty oatmeal cookie loaded with coconut, chocolate chips, and nuts.

1⅔ cups unbleached all-purpose flour

1 teaspoon baking soda

½ teaspoon baking powder

½ teaspoon salt

2 cups old-fashioned (rolled) oats

1¾ cups firmly packed dark brown sugar

½ pound (2 sticks) salted butter, at room temperature

2 large eggs, at room temperature

1 tablespoon water

2 teaspoons pure vanilla extract

1 cup unsweetened coconut flakes (not desiccated; available at natural food stores and online)

1 cup (6 ounces) semisweet chocolate chips

¾ cup toasted and coarsely chopped pecans

1. Position the oven racks in the top third and center of the oven and preheat the oven to 350°F. Line 2 large rimmed baking sheets with parchment paper or silicone baking mats.

2. In a large bowl, whisk together the flour, baking soda, baking powder, and salt. Stir in the oats. In a large bowl, beat the brown sugar and butter with an electric mixer set on high speed until combined, about 1 minute. Beat in the eggs, water, and vanilla. With the mixer on low speed, mix in the flour mixture, just until combined. Stir in the coconut, chocolate chips, and pecans.

3. Using 2 tablespoons per cookie, drop the dough about 2 inches apart onto the prepared baking sheets. (Or use a 1-ounce food portion scoop to scoop the dough onto the baking sheets.) Refrigerate the remaining dough while you bake the first batch.

4. Bake, rotating the positions of the sheets from top to bottom and front to back halfway through baking, until the cookies are lightly browned around the edges and still slightly soft, 13 to 15 minutes. Do not overbake. Let cool on the baking sheets for 5 minutes. Transfer to a wire cooling rack and let cool completely. Repeat with the remaining dough, on cooled baking sheets.

Giant Cowboy Cookies: I prefer to eat two cookies instead of one giant one, but if you like big cookies, use ¼ cup dough per cookie, and space them about 4 inches apart. Bake for about 20 minutes. (Makes about 2 dozen cookies.)

hurricane irene cookies

Makes about 4½ dozen cookies

In 2011, on the morning of Hurricane Irene, I felt that we might need some comforting cookies in the house, so I created a cookie with what was on hand. It turned out fantastic, chubby with lots of good stuff. At first bite, my son Justin remarked, "Oh, don't give these to anyone!"

2½ cups old-fashioned (rolled) oats

1¾ cups unbleached all-purpose flour

1 teaspoon baking soda

¾ teaspoon salt

½ pound (2 sticks) salted butter, softened at room temperature

¾ cup firmly packed dark brown sugar

¼ cup granulated sugar

2 large eggs, at room temperature

2 tablespoons water

1 tablespoon pure vanilla extract

1½ cups (9 ounces) semisweet chocolate chips

1 cup unsweetened coconut flakes (not desiccated; available at natural food stores and online)

1 cup toasted and coarsely chopped pecans

½ cup toffee bits

1. Position the oven racks in the top third and center of the oven and preheat the oven to 325°F. Line 2 large rimmed baking sheets with parchment paper or silicone baking mats.

2. In a medium bowl, whisk together the oats, flour, baking soda, and salt. In a large bowl, beat the butter, brown sugar, and granulated sugar with an electric mixer set on high speed until combined, about 1 minute. One at a time, beat in the eggs, followed by the water and vanilla. With the mixer on low speed, mix in the oat mixture, just until combined. Mix in the chocolate chips, coconut, pecans, and toffee bits.

3. Using 2 tablespoons per cookie, drop the dough 3 inches apart onto the prepared baking sheets. (Or use a 1-ounce food portion scoop to scoop the dough onto the baking sheets.) Refrigerate the remaining dough while you bake the first batch.

4. Bake, rotating the positions of the sheets from top to bottom and front to back halfway through baking, until the edges of the cookies are lightly browned, about 17 minutes. The cookies should be soft; do not overbake. Let cool on the baking sheets for 5 minutes. Transfer to a wire cooling rack and let cool completely. Repeat with the remaining dough, on cooled baking sheets.

chocolate thumbprint cookies

Makes about 6½ dozen cookies

Thumbprint cookies are traditionally flavored with vanilla and filled with fruit jam, but these are chocolate cookies stuffed with more chocolate! They will be a welcome treat on your holiday cookie platter, and they are a perfect hostess gift.

Cookies

2 ounces unsweetened chocolate, finely chopped

2 cups unbleached all-purpose flour

¼ teaspoon salt

½ pound (2 sticks) salted butter, at room temperature

½ cup granulated sugar

⅓ cup firmly packed dark brown sugar

2 large eggs, separated, at room temperature

1 teaspoon pure vanilla extract

3 cups finely chopped pecans

Filling

8 ounces semisweet chocolate, finely chopped

2 teaspoons vegetable oil

1. To make the cookies: Heat the chocolate in a microwave-safe medium bowl on Medium (50% power), stirring at 30-second intervals, until fully melted and smooth. Let stand, stirring occasionally, until tepid, but still fluid.

2. In a medium bowl, whisk together the flour and salt. In a large bowl, beat the butter, granulated sugar, and brown sugar with an electric mixer set on high speed until combined, about 1 minute. One at a time, beat in the egg yolks, followed by the tepid chocolate and the vanilla. With the mixer on low speed, mix in the flour mixture, just until combined. Divide the dough in half and shape each half into a thick disk. Wrap in plastic wrap and refrigerate until chilled, about 2 hours.

3. Position the oven racks in the top third and center of the oven and preheat the oven to 350°F. Line 2 large rimmed baking sheets with parchment paper or silicone baking mats.

4. Using a heaping teaspoon for each, roll the dough into 78 marble-sized balls, putting them in a baking pan or platter. (If you wish, you can cover the balls with plastic wrap and refrigerate for up to 2 days.) Beat the egg whites in a small bowl until foamy. One at a time, dip each ball in the whites, roll in the pecans, and arrange 1½ inches apart on the prepared baking sheets. Refrigerate the remaining balls until ready to bake. Using your thumb (or, if you have long fingernails, the end of a wooden spoon), press an indentation into the center of each cookie.

(continued)

5. Bake, rotating the positions of the sheets from top to bottom and front to back halfway through baking, until the edges of the cookies look set, about 10 minutes. Remove the baking sheets from the oven, and, using your thumb (or the end of the wooden spoon), re-form the center indentation in each cookie. Return to the oven and continue baking until the cookies are crisp, about 10 minutes more. Let cool on the baking sheets for 5 minutes. Transfer to wire cooling racks and let cool completely. Repeat with the remaining balls, egg whites, and pecans, on cooled baking sheets.

6. To make the filling: Heat the chocolate and oil together in a microwave-safe bowl on Medium (50% power), stirring at 30-second intervals, until fully melted and smooth. Let stand, stirring occasionally, until tepid but still fluid.

7. Using a teaspoon, fill the indentations with the chocolate mixture. Let stand until the chocolate sets (you can refrigerate them to speed things up).

chocolate butter balls

Makes about 8½ dozen cookies

These cookies taste like a combination of chocolate shortbread and a Mexican wedding cookie, with a rich flavor. It is a good cookie to make with young friends because it isn't fussy and they'll love rolling the balls.

3½ cups unbleached all-purpose flour

1 cup Dutch-processed cocoa powder

1 cup toasted and skinned hazelnuts, (see page 17) finely ground in a food processor

¼ teaspoon salt

1 pound (4 sticks) salted butter, at room temperature

⅔ cup firmly packed dark brown sugar

¼ cup confectioners' sugar

1 large egg, at room temperature

2 teaspoons pure vanilla extract

2 cups (12 ounces) semisweet chocolate chips

1. In a large bowl, whisk together the flour, cocoa, hazelnuts, and salt. In another large bowl, beat the butter, brown sugar, and confectioners' sugar with an electric mixer set on high speed until combined, about 1 minute. Beat in the egg and vanilla. With the mixer on low speed, mix in the flour mixture, just until combined. Mix in the chocolate chips.

2. Divide the dough into 6 equal pieces. On a cocoa-dusted surface, roll each into a log 15 inches long and 1 inch wide. Place the logs on a baking sheet and refrigerate until firm, about 1 hour. (Or wrap each chilled log in plastic wrap and freeze for up to 1 month. Thaw for 2 hours in the refrigerator before proceeding.)

3. Position the oven racks in the top third and center of the oven and preheat the oven to 350°F. Line 2 large rimmed baking sheets with parchment paper or silicone baking mats.

4. Cut each log into 1-inch slices. Roll each slice into a ball. The dough does not expand through baking, so the balls will be the finished size of the cookies. Arrange the balls 1 inch apart on the prepared baking sheets. Refrigerate the remaining balls while you bake the first batch.

5. Bake, rotating the positions of the sheets from top to bottom and front to back halfway through baking, until the surface of the cookies looks dry and set, about 15 minutes. Let cool on the baking sheets for 5 minutes. Transfer to wire cooling racks and let cool completely. Repeat with the remaining balls, on cooled baking sheets.

white chocolate macadamia nut cookies

Makes 5 dozen cookies

This is one of the top three bestsellers at Tate's Bake Shop. The white chocolate makes the thin and crisp cookie a bit sweeter than others. Use high-quality white chocolate chips that contain cocoa butter, not palm oil or other tropical fats.

2 cups unbleached all-purpose flour

1 teaspoon baking soda

1 teaspoon salt

½ pound (2 sticks) salted butter, at room temperature

¾ cup granulated sugar

¾ cup firmly packed dark brown sugar

2 large eggs, at room temperature

2 teaspoons pure vanilla extract

1½ cups (9 ounces) white chocolate chips

1½ cups coarsely crushed macadamia nuts (put in a zip-tight bag and crush with a rolling pin)

1. Position the oven racks in the top third and center of the oven and preheat the oven to 350°F. Line 2 large rimmed baking sheets with parchment paper or silicone baking mats.

2. In a medium bowl, whisk together the flour, baking soda, and salt. In a large bowl, beat the butter, granulated sugar, and brown sugar with an electric mixer set on high speed until combined, about 1 minute. One at a time, beat in the eggs, followed by the vanilla. With the mixer on low speed, add the flour mixture, and mix just until combined. Mix in the white chocolate chips and crushed macadamia nuts.

3. Using 2 tablespoons per cookie, drop the dough 3 inches apart onto the prepared baking sheets. (Or use a 1-ounce food portion scoop to scoop the dough onto the baking sheets.) Refrigerate the remaining dough while you bake the first batch.

4. Bake, rotating the positions of the sheets from top to bottom and front to back halfway through baking, until the cookies are golden brown, about 20 minutes. Let cool on the baking sheets for 5 minutes. Transfer to a wire cooling rack and let cool completely. Repeat with the remaining dough, using cooled baking sheets.

Giant White Chocolate and Macadamia Nut Cookies. Add 2 cups sweetened coconut flakes and 1 cup (6 ounces) semisweet chocolate chips to the dough along with the white chocolate and macadamia nuts. Cover the bowl and refrigerate for 8 to 12 hours. Use ¼ cup dough per cookie and space 4 inches apart on the baking sheets. Bake for 20 to 22 minutes. (Makes about 3 dozen cookies.)

cranberry, maple, and oatmeal cookies

Makes about 4 dozen cookies

I set out to make a festive cookie for the fall season, but with the vibrant red cranberries, these would also be gorgeous (and delicious) at Christmas time. The contrast of the tart fresh cranberries with the sweet dough is unusual but very pleasing to my palate. If you want sweeter cookies, use dried cranberries.

3 cups old-fashioned (rolled) oats

1¼ cups unbleached all-purpose flour

¾ teaspoon salt

½ teaspoon baking soda

1 cup firmly packed dark brown sugar

12 tablespoons (1½ sticks) salted butter, at room temperature

½ cup Grade B pure maple syrup

1 large egg, at room temperature

1 teaspoon pure vanilla extract

1 teaspoon maple extract (optional)

1½ cups whole fresh cranberries or 1 cup dried cranberries

1 cup toasted and coarsely chopped pecans

1. Position the oven racks in the top third and center of the oven and preheat the oven to 325°F. Line 2 large rimmed baking sheets with parchment paper or silicone baking mats.

2. In a large bowl, whisk together the oats, flour, salt, and baking soda. In a large bowl, beat the brown sugar, butter, and maple syrup with an electric mixer set on high speed until combined, about 1 minute. Beat in the egg, vanilla, and maple extract, if using. With the machine on low speed, mix in the oat mixture, just until combined. Mix in the cranberries and pecans.

3. Using 2 tablespoons per cookie, drop the dough about 2 inches apart onto the prepared baking sheets. (Or use a 1-ounce food portion scoop to scoop the dough onto the baking sheets.) Refrigerate the remaining dough while you bake the first batch.

4. Bake, rotating the positions of the sheets from top to bottom and front to back halfway through baking, until the cookies are lightly browned around the edges and still slightly soft, about 20 minutes. Let cool on the baking sheets for 5 minutes. Transfer to wire cooling racks and let cool completely. Repeat with the remaining dough, on cooled baking sheets.

vanilla madeleines

Makes 2 dozen cookies

These are the famous French shell-shaped cookies that are more like miniature sponge cakes. I think that they are best eaten right after baking, but my friend Judith Rewinski reports they are fine the next day, served for lunch with vanilla yogurt and fresh fruit! Vanilla is the classic flavor, but the orange and lemon zest additions are very good, too.

1 cup granulated sugar

3 large eggs, at room temperature

¼ cup milk

2 teaspoons pure vanilla extract

2 cups unbleached all-purpose flour

1 teaspoon baking powder

8 tablespoons (1 stick) salted butter, melted, and cooled until tepid but still fluid, plus softened butter for the pans

Grated zest of 1 lemon or orange (optional)

Confectioners' sugar for garnish

1. In a medium bowl, beat the granulated sugar and eggs with an electric mixer set on high speed until pale and foamy (not light and fluffy), about 1 minute. Beat in the milk and vanilla. With the mixer on low speed, beat in the flour and baking powder, scraping down the sides of the bowl as needed. Add the melted butter and mix until the batter is very smooth, about 1 minute. Mix in the zest, if using. Cover the bowl and let the batter stand for 2 hours. (The batter can be refrigerated for up to 1 day.)

2. Position a rack in the center of the oven and preheat the oven to 400°F. Lightly butter two 12-mold madeleine pans.

3. Using a 1-ounce (2-tablespoon) food portion scoop, transfer the batter to the molds, letting the batter mound in the center so the madeleines will have their traditional "hump." (You can also use a spoon, but the scoop is much easier.)

4. Bake until a madeleine springs back when pressed on top with a fingertip, about 14 minutes. Immediately remove from the pans. If the madeleines stick, invert the pan and pull them out with a fingertip. Serve warm, or transfer to a wire cooling rack, shell side up, and let cool completely. (Once cool, the madeleines can be transferred to a zip-tight plastic bag and frozen for up to 1 month.) Just before serving, sift confectioners' sugar over the madeleines.

snickerdoodles

Makes 6 dozen cookies

To people who like simple cookies, tender snickerdoodles are better than the fanciest deco-rated cookie. They are all about sugar and spice, but if you like vanilla, add a teaspoon to the dough. This recipe makes a lot of cookies, so have designated recipients before you start baking.

2¾ cups unbleached all-purpose flour

2 teaspoons cream of tartar

1 teaspoon baking soda

½ teaspoon salt

1¾ cups sugar

½ pound (2 sticks) salted butter, at room temperature

2 large eggs, at room temperature

1 tablespoon ground cinnamon

1. In a medium bowl, whisk together the flour, cream of tartar, baking soda, and salt. In a large bowl, beat 1½ cups of the sugar and the butter with an electric mixer set on high speed until combined, about 1 minute. One at a time, beat in the eggs. With the mixer on low speed, mix in the flour mixture, just until combined. Cover the bowl with plastic wrap and refrigerate until the dough is chilled enough to handle easily, at least 2 hours, or up to 1 day.

2. Position the oven racks in the top third and center of the oven and preheat the oven to 350°F. Line 2 large rimmed baking sheets with parchment paper or silicone baking mats.

3. Using about 2 tablespoons for each cookie (you can use a 1-ounce food portion scoop, if you like), roll the dough into balls. In a small bowl, mix together the remaining ¼ cup sugar and the cinnamon. A few at a time, roll the balls in the cinnamon sugar to coat and place in a baking dish. Then arrange the balls of dough 2 inches apart on the prepared baking sheets. Refrigerate the remaining dough balls while you bake the first batch.

4. Bake, switching the positions of the baking sheets from top to bottom and front to back halfway through baking, until the cookies are lightly browned around the edges, about 12 minutes. The cookies should be soft; don't overbake. Let cool on the baking sheet for 5 minutes. Transfer to a wire cooling rack and let cool completely. Repeat with the remaining dough balls, using cooled baking sheets.

pfeffernüsse

Makes 3 dozen cookies

Pfeffernüsse or "pepper nuts" are a traditional Christmas cookie that I don't see as often as I did when growing up. My Mom always brought home a package during the holidays, but they were too spicy for my young taste buds. Now with my mature tastes, I love this spice-heavy, not-too-sweet confection that takes me back to my childhood Christmases.

2 cups unbleached all-purpose flour

2 tablespoons Dutch-processed cocoa powder

1 teaspoon baking powder

¾ teaspoon freshly ground black pepper

½ teaspoon ground anise

½ teaspoon ground cinnamon

¼ teaspoon ground cardamom

¼ teaspoon ground cloves

¼ teaspoon freshly grated nutmeg

¼ teaspoon salt

⅛ teaspoon baking soda

½ cup molasses (not blackstrap)

¼ cup brandy

1 tablespoon fresh lemon juice

8 tablespoons (1 stick) salted butter, at room temperature

⅓ cup firmly packed dark brown sugar

1 large egg, at room temperature

1 teaspoon pure vanilla extract

¾ cup toasted and finely chopped almonds

Grated zest of 2 oranges

Grated zest of 1 lemon

1 cup confectioners' sugar, or as needed

1. In a medium bowl, whisk together the flour, cocoa power, baking powder, pepper, anise, cinnamon, cardamom, cloves, nutmeg, salt, and baking soda. In a small bowl, stir together the molasses, brandy, and lemon juice.

2. In a large bowl, beat the butter and brown sugar with an electric mixer set on high speed until combined, about 1 minute. Mix in the egg and vanilla. Scrape down the sides of the bowl. With the mixer on low speed, mix in the almonds, orange zest, and lemon zest. Using a wooden spoon, stir in the flour mixture, in thirds, alternating with 2 equal additions of the molasses mixture, mixing just until combined. The dough will be sticky but will firm up when chilled. Cover the bowl with plastic wrap. Refrigerate for at least 8 hours, and up to 24 hours.

3. Position the oven racks in the top third and center of the oven and preheat the oven to 350°F. Line 2 baking sheets with parchment paper or silicone baking mats. *(continued)*

4. Using oiled hands, roll the dough into 36 walnut-sized balls. Arrange about 1 inch apart on the baking sheets. Bake, switching the positions of the baking sheets from top to bottom and front to back halfway through baking, until the balls are golden brown, about 12 minutes.

5. Put the confectioners' sugar in a small bowl. A few at a time, roll the warm cookies in the confectioners' sugar to coat. Transfer to a clean baking sheet and let cool completely. Just before serving, roll again in confectioners' sugar.

pumpkin whoopie pies

Makes 26 small whoopie pies

All of a sudden, whoopie pies went from being a specialty of Maine bakeries to a hot menu item around the country. Here is my contribution to the whoopie pie canon, which takes wonderful pumpkin cookies and sandwiches them with a cream cheese filling to make something good even better. You really need a 1-ounce food portion scoop to give these the right appearance—spooning the dough out won't do.

Cookies

2½ cups unbleached all-purpose flour

1 tablespoon ground cinnamon

1 teaspoon baking powder

1 teaspoon ground ginger

½ teaspoon baking soda

½ teaspoon freshly grated nutmeg

½ teaspoon salt

¼ teaspoon ground allspice

1¾ cups firmly packed dark brown sugar

12 tablespoons (1½ sticks) salted butter, at room temperature

¼ cup vegetable oil

2 tablespoons molasses (not blackstrap)

2 large eggs, at room temperature

1 teaspoon pure vanilla extract

One 15-ounce can solid-pack pumpkin

Filling

1 pound cream cheese, at room temperature

4 tablespoons (½ stick) salted butter, at room temperature

2 cups sifted confectioners' sugar

2 teaspoons pure vanilla extract

½ teaspoon maple extract (optional)

¼ cup finely chopped crystallized ginger

1. Position the oven racks in the top third and center of the oven and preheat the oven to 375°F. Line 2 large rimmed baking sheets with parchment paper or silicone baking mats.

2. To make the cookies: In a medium bowl, whisk together the flour, cinnamon, baking powder, ginger, baking soda, nutmeg, salt, and allspice. In a large bowl, beat the brown sugar, butter, oil, and molasses with an electric mixer set on high speed until combined, about 1 minute. One at a time, beat in the eggs, scraping down the bowl after each addition. Add the vanilla and pumpkin and mix well. With the mixer on low speed, mix in the flour mixture, just until combined.

3. Using a 1-ounce (2-tablespoon) food portion scoop, transfer the dough to the baking sheet, placing the cookies 2 inches apart. Refrigerate the remaining dough while you bake the first batch.

4. Bake, rotating the positions of the sheets from top to bottom and front to back halfway through baking, until a cookie springs back when pressed in the center, about 15 minutes. (This is a soft and cakey cookie.) Let cool on the baking sheets for 5 minutes. Transfer to a wire cooling rack and let cool completely. Repeat with the remaining dough, using cooled baking sheets. (The cookies can be individually frozen, then stored in a zip-tight plastic bag for up to 2 months. Thaw before filling.)

5. To make the filling: In a large bowl, beat the cream cheese and butter with an electric mixer on high speed until creamy, about 1 minute. With the mixer on low speed, gradually beat in the confectioners' sugar, followed by the vanilla and maple extract, if using. Beat in the crystallized ginger.

6. To assemble the whoopie pies: For each one, sandwich 2 cookies, flat bottoms facing each other, with 2 tablespoons of the filling (the food scoop works best for portioning the filling). Refrigerate in an airtight container until serving.

linzer heart cookies

These decorative cookies make beautiful and tasty gifts. An important tip: be sure to chop the nuts and chocolate very fine in a food processor (pulse to chop so the friction doesn't warm them), or the dough will be too rough-textured to roll out smoothly. You need a graduated set of heart-shaped cookie cutters to make these.

Cookies

2 cups unbleached all-purpose flour

1 cup cornstarch

¼ teaspoon salt

¾ pound (3 sticks) salted butter, at room temperature

1 cup confectioners' sugar

1 large egg, at room temperature

1 teaspoon pure vanilla extract

2 cups toasted, skinned and very finely chopped hazelnuts (see page 17 and the headnote)

6 ounces bittersweet chocolate, very finely chopped

½ cup seedless raspberry jam

½ cup confectioners' sugar for sifting

1. Sift the flour, cornstarch, and salt into a medium bowl. In a large bowl, beat the butter and confectioners' sugar with an electric mixer set on high speed until combined, about 1 minute . Beat in the egg and vanilla, scraping down the sides of the bowl as needed. With the mixer on low speed, mix in the flour mixture, just until combined. Mix in the hazelnuts and chocolate.

2. Gather up the dough and shape it into a flat disk. Wrap in plastic wrap and refrigerate until chilled, at least 2 hours. (The dough can be refrigerated for up to 1 day. Let stand at room temperature for 10 minutes to soften slightly before rolling.)

3. Line 2 large rimmed baking sheets with parchment paper or silicone baking mats. On a lightly floured work surface, roll out the dough to a round about ¼ inch thick. Use a 3½-inch heart-shaped cookie cutter to cut out the cookies as close as possible to avoid excess scraps. Arrange the hearts about 1 inch apart on the prepared baking sheets. Gather up the dough scraps and gently knead together, and cut out more cookies. If the dough becomes too soft to roll out, refrigerate until chilled. You should have 40 cookies. Refrigerate for 30 minutes to 1 hour. (Don't skip this step or the cookies will lose their shape during baking.)

(continued)

4. Position the oven racks in the top third and center of the oven and preheat the oven to 325°F.

5. Use a 1-inch heart-shaped cookie cutter to cut out the centers of 20 cookies. These will be the cookie tops. (You can bake the mini hearts to nibble on later. Don't throw away or reroll.) Bake, switching the position of the baking sheets from top to bottom and front to back halfway through baking, until the cookies begin to brown, 20 to 25 minutes. Sift some of the ½ cup of confectioners' sugar over the hot cut-out cookies Let cool completely on the baking sheets.

6. Spread the jam on the cookie bottoms, leaving an ⅛-inch border around the edges. Add the tops, sugared sides up, and press together gently. Just before serving, sift the remaining confectioners' sugar over the cookies.

shortbread

Makes 32 cookies

Shortbread reminds me of nothing more than crisp butter. As the butter is front and center, use the very best brand, perhaps an imported variety. I start with the classic version here, then offer several variations to suit your fancy. All are unfussy, freeze well (I keep some in a zip-tight bag to serve with fresh fruit), and ship well.

> 3 cups unbleached all-purpose flour
> ¾ cup granulated sugar
> ¾ pound (3 sticks) cold salted butter, cut into ½-inch cubes

1. Position an oven rack in the center of the oven and preheat the oven to 325°F. Line the bottom and 2 short ends of a 13-by-9-inch baking pan with a 20-inch length of aluminum foil, pleating the foil as needed, and letting the excess foil hang over the ends. Lightly butter the foil.

2. In the bowl of a standing, heavy-duty electric mixer, combine the flour and sugar. Add the butter and mix with the paddle attachment on low speed until the mixture looks crumbly, about 1½ minutes. (Add any of the variation flavorings listed below at this point.) Press firmly and evenly into the prepared pan.

3. Bake until the shortbread is golden brown on top and slightly darker around the edges, about 1 hour. Cut into 32 pieces while still warm. (If cooled before cutting, the shortbread will break.) Let cool completely in the pan on a wire cooling rack.

4. Run a dinner knife around the inside of the pan to loosen the shortbread. Lift up the foil "handles" to remove the shortbread from the pan. Cut through the previously cut marks into 32 pieces.

Lemon Ginger Shortbread: Add 1 cup chopped crystallized ginger, 1 cup minced candied lemon peel (or the grated zest of 1 lemon), and 2 tablespoons fresh lemon juice.

Brown Sugar Ginger Shortbread: Substitute 1 cup firmly packed dark brown sugar for the granulated sugar, and add 1 cup crystallized ginger.

Chocolate Chip Shortbread: Add 1 cup (6 ounces) miniature chocolate chips.

Pecan Shortbread: Add 1 cup toasted and finely chopped pecans.

chocolate-dipped orange shortbread

Makes about 4½ dozen cookies

Orange shortbread is a very versatile cookie. Dipped in chocolate, it has a tailored appearance for the most elegant occasion. The dough can also be cut into stars, trees, or other shapes to decorate as holiday cookies. This recipe yields a large batch, so freeze some of them to dip at another time, if you wish.

Shortbread

3 cups unbleached all-purpose flour, plus more for rolling and cutting out the dough

1½ teaspoons baking powder

¼ teaspoon salt

½ pound (2 sticks) salted butter, at room temperature

1 cup firmly packed dark brown sugar

1 large egg

Grated zest of 1 orange

3 tablespoons fresh orange juice

1 teaspoon pure vanilla extract

6 ounces semisweet chocolate, coarsely chopped

(continued)

1. To make the shortbread, in a medium bowl, whisk together the flour, baking powder, and salt. In a large bowl, beat the butter and brown sugar with an electric mixer set on high speed until combined, about 1 minute. Beat in the egg, followed by the orange zest, orange juice, and vanilla. With the mixer on low speed, mix in the flour mixture, just until combined.

2. Divide the dough in half and shape each half into a thick disk. Wrap in plastic wrap and refrigerate until chilled, about 2 hours. (The dough can be refrigerated for up to 2 days. If it is too firm to roll out, let stand at room temperature for 15 to 30 minutes to soften slightly.)

3. Position the oven racks in the top third and center of the oven and preheat the oven to 325°F. Line 2 large rimmed baking sheets with parchment paper or silicone baking mats.

4. Working with 1 disk at a time, briefly knead the dough on a lightly floured work surface until smooth. Roll out the dough ⅛ inch thick. Dip a 2½-inch round cookie cutter or another shape of a similar size in flour and cut out cookies, cutting them as close together as possible to avoid excess scraps. Arrange the rounds about 1 inch apart on the prepared baking sheets. Gather up the dough scraps and gently knead together, and cut out more cookies. If the dough becomes too soft to roll out, refrigerate until chilled. Refrigerate any remaining dough while you bake the first batch.

5. Bake, rotating the positions of the sheets from top to bottom and front to back halfway through baking, until the cookies are lightly browned on the edges and bottoms, about 20 minutes. The cookie tops will not brown, but do not underbake them, or they lack flavor. Let cool on the baking sheets for 5 minutes. Transfer to wire cooling racks and let cool completely. Repeat with the remaining dough, on cooled baking sheets.

6. To dip the cookies, line baking sheets with parchment paper or baking mats. Put the chocolate in a microwave-safe medium bowl. Heat the chocolate on Medium (50% power), stirring at 30-second intervals, until fully melted. Let stand, stirring occasionally, until the chocolate has cooled to 89°F on an instant-read thermometer. Place the bowl in another bowl of hot tap water to keep it warm enough for dipping, being careful not to splash water into the melted chocolate.

7. One at a time, dip one half of each cookie into the chocolate. Drag the bottom of the cookie across the rim of the bowl to remove excess chocolate, and place the cookie on the baking sheet. If the chocolate cools and thickens, warm in the microwave for 15 seconds at Medium (50% power). Let the cookies stand until the chocolate sets and they can be easily lifted from the baking sheet, about 1 hour.

chocolate shortbread hearts

Makes about 4½ dozen cookies

This beautiful dark cookie really holds its shape during baking, so you'll get perfect hearts, just right for giving to friends on Valentine's Day. For an easy decoration, put some melted white chocolate in a small plastic bag, snip off a corner of the bag, and pipe out the chocolate onto the cookies. Or dip them as instructed for the Chocolate-Dipped Orange Shortbread on page 132.

2¾ cups unbleached all-purpose flour, plus more for rolling out the dough

¾ cup Dutch-processed cocoa powder, plus more for cutting out the dough

1 teaspoon baking powder

½ teaspoon salt

½ pound (2 sticks) salted butter, at room temperature

1½ cups firmly packed dark brown sugar

2 large eggs, at room temperature

1½ teaspoons pure vanilla extract

1. In a medium bowl, whisk together 2¾ cups flour, ¾ cup cocoa, the baking powder, and salt. In a large bowl, beat the butter and brown sugar with an electric mixer set on high speed until combined, about 1 minute. One at a time, beat in the eggs, followed by the vanilla. With the machine on low speed, mix in the flour mixture, just until combined.

2. Divide the dough in half and shape each half into a thick disk. Wrap in plastic wrap and refrigerate until chilled, about 2 hours. (The dough can be refrigerated for up to 2 days. If it is too firm to roll out, let stand at room temperature for 15 to 30 minutes to soften slightly.)

3. Position the racks in the top third and center of the oven and preheat the oven to 325°F. Line 2 large rimmed baking sheets with parchment paper or silicone baking mats.

4. Very lightly dust a work surface with flour (to avoid streaks of flour on the dough). Working with 1 disk at a time, roll out the dough ¼ inch thick. Dip a 2½-inch heart cookie cutter into cocoa and cut out cookies, cutting them as close together as possible to avoid excess scraps. Arrange the cookies about 1 inch apart on the prepared baking sheets. Gather up the dough scraps and gently knead together, roll out again, and cut out more cookies. Refrigerate any remaining dough while you bake the first batch.

5. Bake, rotating the positions of the sheets from top to bottom and front to back halfway through baking, until the edges of the cookies look set, about 15 minutes. Let cool on the baking sheets for 5 minutes. Transfer to wire cooling racks and let cool completely. Repeat with the remaining dough and scraps on cooled baking sheets.

lime sugar cookies

Makes about 3½ dozen cookies

These cookies are deliciously simple. The ingredients combine to give them a truly melt-in-your-mouth quality that will have you going back for more. During the summer, they go well with fresh fruit salad, and are the perfect finish for a seafood dinner.

1½ cups unbleached all-purpose flour

½ cup white or brown rice flour
(available at natural food stores
and many supermarkets)

¼ teaspoon salt

½ pound (2 sticks) salted butter,
softened at room temperature

1 cup confectioners' sugar

Grated zest of 2 limes

2 tablespoons fresh lime juice

1 teaspoon lime oil

1. In a small bowl, whisk together the all-purpose flour, rice flour, and salt. In a large bowl, beat the butter and ½ cup of the confectioners' sugar with an electric mixer set on high speed until combined, about 1 minute. Beat in the lime zest, lime juice, and lime oil. With the mixer on low speed, mix in the flour mixture, just until combined.

2. Gather up the dough into a thick disk. Wrap in plastic wrap and refrigerate until chilled and firm, about 2 hours. (The dough can be refrigerated for up to 1 day. Let stand at room temperature for 10 minutes to soften slightly before rolling.)

3. Position an oven rack in the center of the oven and preheat the oven to 350°F. Line a large rimmed baking sheet with parchment paper or a silicone baking mat.

4. Divide the dough into 42 equal pieces and roll into balls. The dough does not expand through baking, so the balls will be the finished size of the cookies. Arrange the balls 1 inch apart on the prepared baking sheet.

5. Bake the cookies until the tops are golden brown and the bottoms are lightly browned, about 17 minutes. Sift some of the remaining ½ cup confectioners' sugar over the hot cookies on the baking sheet. Let cool completely on the baking sheet. Repeat with the remaining dough, on a cooled sheet.

6. Put the remaining confectioners' sugar in a small paper bag. A few at a time, shake the cookies in the bag to thoroughly coat with the sugar.

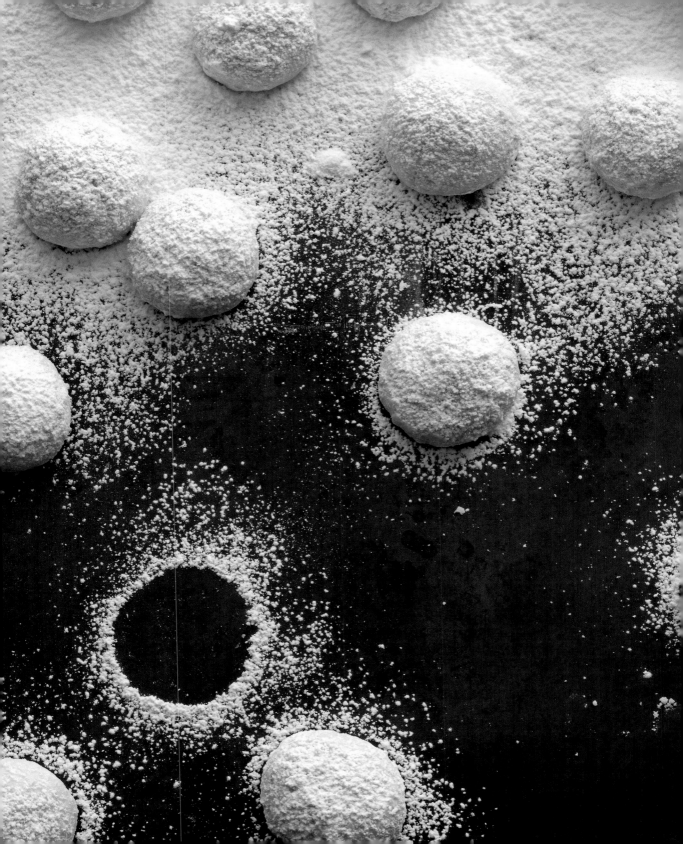

graham crackers

Makes 4 dozen crackers

This recipe took me several attempts to get just it just right. Every morning I would wake up and make a new batch, each time getting closer to the taste and texture I wanted. If you like store-bought graham crackers, wait until you try this homemade version. They are thin and crisp, but not too hard, with that graham flavor we all love. These keep well in the freezer, so make a batch to have ready for your summertime s'mores or just for snacking.

⅓ cup honey

⅓ cup water

1 teaspoon pure vanilla extract

1⅓ cups unbleached all-purpose flour

1¼ cups whole wheat flour

¾ cup firmly packed dark brown sugar

1 teaspoon baking soda

¾ teaspoon salt

6 tablespoons (¾ stick) cold salted butter, cut into small pieces

1. In a small bowl, combine the honey, water, and vanilla. In a food processor, pulse the all-purpose flour, whole wheat flour, brown sugar, baking soda, and salt until combined. Add the butter and pulse until the mixture resembles coarse meal. Add the honey mixture and pulse just until combined. Gather up the dough and divide it into 3 pieces. Shape each one into a thick rectangle. Wrap each one in plastic wrap and refrigerate until chilled but not hard, about 1½ hours.

2. Position a rack in the center of the oven and preheat the oven to 300°F. Line a large rimmed baking sheet with parchment paper or a silicone baking mat.

3. Lightly flour the work surface. One piece at a time, keeping the remaining dough refrigerated, roll out the dough into a rectangle about ⅛ inch thick, no thicker. Using a pizza cutter or large knife, cut into 2-inch squares. Using a metal spatula, transfer the crackers to the prepared baking sheets. (The crackers won't spread during baking, so you can put them close together.) Using the tines of a fork, prick 3 evenly spaced decorative sets of holes in each cracker.

4. Bake, 1 sheet of crackers at a time, until slightly firm when pressed with a finger tip and the edges begin to brown, 25 minutes. (While it is time consuming to bake the crackers one sheet at a time, it does make a difference, because the crackers will cook too quickly if placed too high or too low in the oven, and acquire a burned taste without looking burned.) Let cool on the pan for 3 minutes, then transfer to a wire cooling rack to cool completely. Roll out and bake the remaining crackers.

key lime squares

Makes 16 bars

These creamy bars were a hit from the first day that we sold them at the bake shop. They taste like Key lime pie, but the cream cheese gives the filling a bit more body. If you can find small Key limes, use them, but this works fine with standard Persian limes. The ginger crust adds an interesting, unexpected twist on the traditional graham cracker crust.

Softened butter for the baking pan

Ingredients for Gingersnap Cookie Crust or Sugar Cookie Crust with Ginger (page 100)

4 ounces cream cheese, at room temperature

4 large egg yolks

One 14-ounce sweetened condensed milk

Grated zest of 4 Key limes or 2 regular limes

½ cup fresh lime juice, preferably from Key limes

1. Position an oven rack in the center of the oven and preheat the oven to 350°F. Lightly butter a 9-inch square baking pan. Line the bottom and 2 opposite ends of the pan with an 18-inch length of aluminum foil, pleating the foil to fit, and letting the excess foil hang over the sides. Lightly butter the foil.

2. Mix the cookie crust and press it firmly and evenly into the pan. Bake until the crust smells sweet and toasty, about 10 minutes. Remove from the oven.

3. In a large bowl, beat the cream cheese with an electric mixer set on high speed until smooth. Beat in the egg yolks, scraping down the sides of the bowl as needed. Beat in the condensed milk and lime zest, followed by the lime juice. Pour into the warm crust.

4. Bake until the edges of the bars are beginning to brown, about 15 minutes. Let cool completely in the pan on a wire cooling rack. Refrigerate until chilled, about 2 hours.

5. Run a dinner knife around the edges of the pan to release the bars. Lift up the foil "handles" to remove the bars. Cut into 16 squares.

pecan squares

Makes 2 dozen bars

The crunchy shortbread layer with the sweet caramelized pecan topping makes a delicious snack. Or serve it for dessert in larger portions, topped with vanilla or caramel ice cream.

Shortbread Layer
Softened butter for the pan
1½ cups unbleached all-purpose flour
12 tablespoons (1½ sticks) cold salted butter, cut into ½-inch cubes, plus more for the pan
⅓ cup granulated sugar

Topping
10 tablespoons (1¼ sticks) salted butter, cut into tablespoons
½ cup firmly packed dark brown sugar
¼ cup honey
¼ cup Grade B pure maple syrup
¼ cup heavy cream
3½ cups coarsely chopped pecans

1. Position an oven rack in the center of the oven and preheat the oven to 350°F. Butter a 13-by-9-inch baking pan. Line the bottom and the 2 short ends with a 20-inch-long piece of aluminum foil, pleating the foil to fit and letting the excess foil hang over the ends. Lightly butter the foil.

2. To make the shortbread layer: In a medium bowl, mix the flour, butter, and sugar with an electric mixer set on low speed just until combined and crumbly. Do not mix into a dough; it should remain crumbly. Press firmly and evenly into the prepared pan. Bake until golden brown, about 30 minutes. Remove from the oven and let stand on a wire cooling rack. Leave the oven on.

3. To make the topping: In a medium saucepan, bring the butter, brown sugar, honey, maple syrup, and heavy cream to a boil, stirring until the butter melts. Boil for 2 minutes. Remove from the heat and stir in the pecans. Pour and spread the pecan mixture over the crust.

4. Return to the oven and bake until the pecan mixture is bubbling and golden brown around the edges, about 30 minutes. Let cool completely in the pan on a wire cooling rack.

5. Run a dinner knife around the edges of the shortbread to release it. Lift up the foil "handles" and remove the shortbread from the pan. Using a long sharp knife, cut into 24 rectangles.

cranberry sauce crumb bars

Makes 2 dozen cookies

After Thanksgiving, you can make soup from many of the leftovers, but the cranberry sauce often remains neglected in the refrigerator. Since I abhor anything going to waste, I made these crumb bars using cranberry sauce as the filling. This works only with sweet, thick sauce, not a cranberry chutney with savory ingredients like onions or garlic. If you don't have cranberry sauce, substitute your favorite fruit preserves.

Softened butter for the pan

1¼ cups old-fashioned (rolled) oats

1 cup unbleached all-purpose flour

¾ cup firmly packed dark brown sugar

⅔ cup whole wheat flour

½ teaspoon ground cinnamon

½ teaspoon baking powder

½ teaspoon baking soda

½ teaspoon salt

13 tablespoons (1½ sticks plus 1 tablespoon), cold salted butter, cut into ½-inch cubes

1 cup toasted and coarsely chopped pecans

1½ cups homemade cranberry sauce

1. Position a rack in the center of the oven and preheat the oven to 350°F. Butter a 13-by-9-inch baking pan. Line the bottom and the 2 short ends with a 20-inch-long piece of aluminum foil, pleating the foil to fit, letting the excess foil hang over the ends. Butter the foil.

2. In a large bowl, stir together the oats, all-purpose flour, brown sugar, whole wheat flour, cinnamon, baking powder, baking soda, and salt. Add the butter and work it in with your fingertips until the mixture is well combined and crumbly. (You can also do this in the bowl of a heavy-duty standing electric mixer with the paddle attachment on medium-low speed.) Work in the pecans. Press half of the crumb mixture firmly and evenly into the prepared pan.

3. Bake until the crumb layer is just turning golden, about 20 minutes. Remove from the oven. Spread the cranberry sauce over the crumb layer. Sprinkle the remaining crumb mixture evenly over the sauce and press it gently into the sauce.

4. Bake until the edges are beginning to brown and the filling feels set when the topping is pressed in the center with a fingertip, about 45 minutes. Transfer to a wire cooling rack and let cool completely in the pan.

5. Run a dinner knife around the inside of the pan to loosen the bars. Lift up the foil "handles" to remove them from the pan. Cut into 24 bars.

date crumb bars

Makes 16 bars

These may look like the average date bar, but don't be fooled: They are the best date bars you will ever make. Too often, date bars are sugar bombs. Here all of the ingredients—oats, walnuts, ginger, and naturally sweet dates—stand out.

Softened butter for the pan

2 cups packed pitted and coarsely chopped dates

1½ cups water

1 teaspoon pure vanilla extract

2 cups old-fashioned (rolled) oats

1 cup unbleached all-purpose flour

¾ cup firmly packed dark brown sugar

½ cup whole wheat flour

1½ teaspoons ground cinnamon

½ teaspoon baking soda

⅛ teaspoon salt

1½ cups coarsely chopped walnuts

½ cup finely chopped crystallized ginger

½ pound (2 sticks) salted butter, cut into tablespoons, at room temperature

1. In a small saucepan, bring the dates and water to a boil over medium heat. Reduce the heat to medium-low and simmer, stirring occasionally, until the dates are tender and cooked into a thick jam, 15 minutes. Remove from the heat and stir in the vanilla. Let the filling cool completely.

2. Preheat the oven to 350°F. Lightly butter a 9-inch square baking pan. Line the bottom and 2 opposite ends of the pan with an 18-inch length of aluminum foil, pleating the foil to fit, and letting the excess foil hang over the sides. Lightly butter the foil.

3. In a large bowl, stir together the oats, all-purpose flour, brown sugar, whole wheat flour, cinnamon, baking soda, and salt. Stir in the walnuts and ginger. Add the butter and work it in with your fingertips until the mixture is well combined and crumbly. (You can also do this in the bowl of a heavy-duty standing electric mixer with the paddle attachment on medium-low speed.)

4. Press half of the crumb mixture firmly and evenly into the prepared pan. Spread the date filling on top. Sprinkle the remaining crumb mixture evenly over the top and press gently into the filling.

(continued)

5. Bake until the edges are beginning to brown and the filling feels set when the topping is pressed in the center with a fingertip, about 1 hour. Transfer to a wire cooling rack and let cool completely in the pan. Run a knife around the inside of the pan to loosen the bars. Lift up the foil "handles" to remove them from the pan. Cut into 16 bars.

milk chocolate brownies

Makes 16 brownies

I don't bake with milk chocolate often, but each time I do, I am pleasantly surprised how delicious it is. (You can probably tell from my recipes that I am a dark chocolate fan!) These brownies are moist, rich, and very chocolaty.

8 tablespoons (1 stick) salted butter, cut into tablespoons, plus softened butter for the pan

9 ounces milk chocolate, finely chopped

½ cup sugar

2 large eggs, at room temperature

1 teaspoon pure vanilla extract

¾ cup unbleached all-purpose flour

1 tablespoon natural cocoa powder

Pinch of salt

1. Position an oven rack in the center of the oven and preheat the oven to 350°F. Lightly butter a 9-inch square pan. Line the bottom and 2 opposite sides of the pan with an 18-inch length of aluminum foil, pleating the foil to fit and letting the excess foil hang over the sides. Lightly butter the foil.

2. In a small saucepan, melt the butter over medium heat. Remove from the heat. Add the chocolate and let stand for 1 minute. Stir until the chocolate is melted and smooth. Scrape into a medium bowl and let cool slightly.

3. Add the sugar, eggs, and vanilla to the chocolate mixture and mix well. Add the flour, cocoa, and salt and stir until smooth. Spread evenly in the prepared pan.

4. Bake until a wooden toothpick inserted into the center of the brownies comes out with moist crumbs, about 20 minutes. Transfer the pan to a wire cooling rack and let cool completely. Run a dinner knife around the inside of the pan to loosen the brownies. Lift up the foil "handles" to remove the brownies from the pan. Cut into 16 squares.

chestnut brownies

Makes 16 small brownies

When the holidays come around, take your everyday baking up a notch. These brownies look like familiar chocolate brownies, but the chestnut spread makes them special enough to give as a gift. To make this gluten-free, substitute chestnut flour, available at Italian grocers and many natural food stores, for the all-purpose flour. These brownies cut best when chilled.

6 tablespoons (¾ stick) salted butter, cut into chunks, plus softened butter for the pan

6 ounces semisweet chocolate, finely chopped

1 cup sugar

½ cup sweetened chestnut spread (*crème de marrons,* available at specialty grocers)

1 teaspoon pure vanilla extract

½ teaspoon instant espresso powder

¼ teaspoon salt

2 large eggs, at room temperature

1 cup unbleached all-purpose flour

2 tablespoons natural cocoa powder

1. Position an oven rack in the center of the oven and preheat the oven to 325°F. Lightly butter an 8-inch square pan. Line the bottom and 2 opposite ends of the pan with an 18-inch length of aluminum foil, pleating the foil to fit, and letting the excess foil hang over the sides. Lightly butter the foil.

2. In a small saucepan, melt the butter over medium heat. Remove from the heat. Add the chocolate and let stand for 2 minutes. Stir until the chocolate is melted and smooth. Scrape into a medium bowl and let cool slightly.

3. Add the sugar, chestnut spread, vanilla, espresso powder, and salt to the chocolate mixture and stir well. One at a time, stir in the eggs, stirring well after each addition. Scrape down the sides of the bowl. Add the flour and cocoa and stir until smooth, scraping down the sides of the bowl as needed. Spread evenly in the prepared pan.

4. Bake until a wooden toothpick inserted into the center of the brownies comes out with moist crumbs, about 30 minutes. Do not overbake. Transfer the pan to a wire cooling rack and let cool completely. Cover with plastic wrap and refrigerate until chilled, at least 2 hours.

5. Run a dinner knife around the inside of the pan to loosen the brownies. Lift up the foil "handles" to remove the brownies from the pan, and cut into 16 squares.

guinness brownies

Makes 16 brownies

I made these to fit into the tradition of downing a pint on St. Patrick's Day. You can eat them out of hand, or serve as a plated dessert with Baileys Whipped Cream (page 200) or vanilla ice cream drizzled with Baileys Irish Cream. I gave my test batch to my son and he texted me, "I can taste the Guinness, they are really good!"

6 tablespoons (¾ stick) salted butter, cut into tablespoons, plus softened butter for the pan

12 ounces high-quality milk chocolate, finely chopped

¾ cup unbleached all-purpose flour

¾ cup natural cocoa powder

¼ teaspoon salt

4 large eggs, at room temperature

¾ cup granulated sugar

¼ cup firmly packed dark brown sugar

1¼ cups stout, preferably Guinness (this is ¼ cup short of a 12-ounce bottle, which you can drink as the baker's treat, if you wish)

1 cup (6 ounces) semisweet chocolate chips

1. Position an oven rack in the center of the oven and preheat the oven to 325°F. Lightly butter a 9-inch square baking pan. Line the bottom and 2 opposite ends of the pan with an 18-inch length of aluminum foil, pleating the foil to fit, and letting the excess foil hang over the sides. Lightly butter the foil.

2. In a small saucepan, melt the butter over medium heat. Remove from the heat, add the chocolate, and let stand for 1 minute. Stir until the chocolate is melted and smooth. Scrape into a medium bowl and let cool slightly.

3. In a small bowl, whisk together the flour, cocoa, and salt. In a large bowl, beat the eggs, granulated sugar, and brown sugar with an electric mixer set on high speed until combined, about 1 minute. With the mixer on low speed, beat in the chocolate mixture. Scrape down the sides of the bowl. With the mixer still on low speed, add the flour mixture, followed by the stout, scraping down the sides of the bowl as needed. Spread evenly in the prepared pan. Sprinkle the chocolate chips evenly over the batter.

4. Bake until a wooden toothpick inserted into the center of the brownies comes out with moist crumbs, about 50 minutes. (This brownie takes longer than the basic version, but do not overbake.) Transfer the pan to a wire cooling rack and let cool completely. Run a knife around the inside of the pan to loosen the brownies. Lift up the foil "handles" to remove them from the pan. Cut into 16 squares.

almond biscotti, franco's way

Makes 2½ dozen biscotti

My friend Franco Biscardi is an incredible interior designer and an amazing, authentic Italian cook. He trained to be a chef but decided that he prefers cooking just for family and friends. Last year he started a blog, www.italian-ate.com. I read it every morning, as it makes me feel like I had dinner with him. His biscotti are classically simple, slightly sweet, and the perfect accompaniment to espresso or vin santo.

3¼ cup unbleached all-purpose flour

2 cups salted whole almonds, finely ground in the food processor

1 tablespoon baking powder

1 cup plus 2 tablespoons Demerara or other raw sugar

½ cup pure olive oil (not extra virgin)

3 large eggs, at room temperature

Grated zest of ½ lemon

1. Preheat the oven to 375°F. Line a large rimmed baking sheet with parchment paper or a silicone baking mat.

2. In a large bowl, whisk together the flour, ground almonds, and baking powder. In the bowl of a heavy-duty standing electric mixer fitted with the paddle attachment, mix 1 cup of the sugar, oil, eggs, and lemon zest on low speed just until combined. With the mixer still on low speed, mix in the flour mixture, just until combined. (Or whisk the sugar, oil, eggs, and lemon zest together in a large bowl. Gradually stir in the flour mixture, using your hands to mix if the dough becomes too stiff.)

3. Gather the dough together and divide it in half. Working on the prepared baking sheet, shape each half into a 14-inch-long log about 3 inches wide and ¾ inch thick, spacing the logs well apart. The dough will be crumbly, but will hold together as you press the logs into shape. Sprinkle each one with 1 tablespoon of the remaining Demerara sugar.

4. Bake until the dough logs are lightly browned, about 25 minutes. Let cool on the baking sheet for at least 15 minutes, preferably 1 hour.

5. Preheat the oven again, if necessary. Line a second large baking sheet with parchment paper or a silicone baking mat. With a long serrated knife, cut the logs straight across into ¾-inch-thick slices. Arrange the biscotti cut side down on the baking sheet. Bake, flipping the cookies after 7 minutes, until they are crisp and golden brown, about 15 minutes. Let cool for 5 minutes on the baking sheet. Transfer to wire cooling racks and let cool completely.

chocolate almond biscotti

Makes about 3½ dozen biscotti

These biscotti really taste like chocolate, unlike some that I have had that look rich but lack a strong "bang" of chocolate flavor. Search out ammonium carbonate (available at www.amazon.com), as this Old World leavening makes very crisp biscotti.

2 cups unbleached all-purpose flour

½ cup Dutch-processed cocoa powder

1 tablespoon instant espresso powder

½ teaspoon ammonium carbonate or baking powder

¾ teaspoon salt

8 tablespoons (1 stick) salted butter, at room temperature

½ cup granulated sugar

½ cup firmly packed dark brown sugar

2 large eggs, at room temperature

1 teaspoon pure vanilla extract

1 cup toasted and chopped natural almonds

1 cup (6 ounces) semisweet chocolate chips

1. Position an oven rack in the center of the oven and preheat the oven to 350°F. Line a large rimmed baking sheet with parchment paper or a silicone baking mat.

2. In a medium bowl, whisk together the flour, cocoa powder, espresso powder, ammonium carbonate, and salt. In a large bowl, beat the butter, granulated sugar, and brown sugar with an electric mixer set on high speed until combined, about 1 minute. One at a time, beat in the eggs, then the vanilla. Scrape down the sides of the bowl. With the mixer on low speed, add the flour mixture, just until combined. Mix in the almonds and chocolate chips.

3. Divide the dough in half. On a lightly floured work surface, shape each half into a 12-inch-long cylinder, then pat into a log about 1 inch thick and 2 inches wide. Place well apart on the prepared baking sheet.

4. Bake until the dough logs look dry on the surface and feel firm but not hard when pressed with a fingertip, about 30 minutes. Let cool on the baking sheet for at least 15 minutes. (The logs can be cooled completely and left at room temperature for up to 4 hours. Or wrap each cooled log in plastic wrap and aluminum foil and freeze for up to 1 month; thaw in the refrigerator before proceeding.)

5. With a long serrated knife, cut the logs straight across into ¾-inch-thick slices. Arrange the biscotti close together cut side down on the baking sheet. Bake, flipping the biscotti after 10 minutes, until crisp, about 20 minutes. Let cool completely on the baking sheet.

chapter 5

party cakes
& cupcakes

TIPS FOR PARTY CAKES AND CUPCAKES

✳ The ingredients for cake batters are mixed most efficiently if they are all at room temperature. This is especially important for eggs, which tend to look curdled if added to the creamed butter and sugar mixture when cold. The butter should be at room temperature, but not squishy or shiny.

✳ It's better if the milk or buttermilk is not ice-cold, either, but that isn't mandatory. If you remember, let stand at room temperature while the oven is preheating, or microwave at low power just until the milk loses its chill.

✳ Cake layers can be baked well ahead of time. Cool completely on wire cooling racks, then wrap them tightly in plastic wrap and freeze for up to 1 month. I always have frozen cake layers ready for frosting.

✳ The most common tool for testing a cake for doneness is a wooden toothpick—if the toothpick is inserted in the cake and it comes out clean, the cake is done. But I also like a cake tester, a thin wire skewer that is specific for this job. Store the tester where you can find it easily.

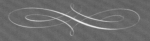

caramel cake

Makes 12 servings

When my my book club read The Help *by Kathryn Stockett, it drove me to recreate the character Minny's caramel cake. This cake is best to serve on the day it is made.*

Softened butter and all-purpose flour
  for the pan

1½ cups cake flour (not self-rising)

1½ teaspoons baking powder

½ teaspoon salt

¼ cup milk

2 teaspoons pure vanilla extract

2 cups firmly packed dark brown sugar

8 tablespoons (1 stick) salted butter,
  at room temperature

4 large eggs, separated, at room temperature

1 cup toasted and finely chopped pecans
  (optional)

Caramel Icing (page 198)

Whipped Cream (page 200)

1. Position an oven rack in the center of the oven and preheat the oven to 350°F. Lightly butter two 8-by-2-inch round cake pans and line the bottoms with waxed or parchment paper. Dust the insides with flour and tap out the excess.

2. To make the cake: Sift together the cake flour, baking powder, and salt into a medium bowl. In a glass measuring cup, stir together the milk and vanilla. In a large bowl, beat the brown sugar and butter together with an electric mixer set on high speed until pale, about 3 minutes. One at a time, beat in the egg yolks, beating well after each addition. With the mixer on low speed, add the flour mixture in thirds, alternating with the milk mixture in 2 equal additions, beating until smooth, scraping down the sides of the bowls as needed. Using clean beaters, in a large bowl, beat the egg whites until soft peaks form. Stir about one-quarter of the whites into the batter to loosen it. Fold in the remaining whites. Fold in the pecans, if using. Divide the batter between the prepared pans and smooth the tops.

3. Bake until the cakes spring back when pressed with your fingertip, about 25 minutes. Let cool in the pans on wire cooling racks for 10 minutes. Run a dinner knife around the insides of the pans to release the cakes, invert onto the racks, and remove the pans and paper. Turn the cakes right side up on the racks and let cool completely.

4. Place a dab of icing on a serving plate. Place 1 cake layer, flat side up, on the plate. Using a metal icing spatula, spread it with about 1 cup of the icing. Place the second cake layer, flat side down, on top. Pour the remaining icing over the top of the cake, and spread it with the spatula so icing drips down the sides of the cake. (Do not frost the sides of the cake). Let stand until the icing sets. Serve each slice with a dollop of whipped cream.

cherry chip party cake

Makes 12 servings

When I was a kid, I loved cherry chip cake made from cake mix. Here is my from-scratch version. (These days, I must make it from scratch because I cannot be seen buying cake mix at my local market!) Tall, fluffy, moist, and sweet, it is even better than I remember it. If you wish, use the Pink Fluffy Icing on page 197 to give the cake a pink coating to make it appropriate for Valentine's Day or a little girl's birthday.

Softened butter and all-purpose flour
for the pans

3 cups cake flour (not self-rising),
preferably unbleached

1 tablespoon baking powder

½ teaspoon salt

¾ cup milk

¾ cup drained and chopped maraschino
cherries, plus ¼ cup cherry juice
from the jar

½ teaspoon almond extract

½ teaspoon pure vanilla extract

2 cups sugar

½ pound (2 sticks) salted butter,
at room temperature

5 large egg whites, at room temperature

Fluffy Vanilla Frosting (page 196)

12 maraschino cherries, drained, for garnish

1. Position an oven rack in the center of the oven and preheat the oven to 350°F. Lightly butter two 9-by-2-inch round cake pans and line the bottoms with waxed or parchment paper. Dust the insides with flour and tap out the excess.

2. To make the cake: Sift the cake flour, baking powder, and salt into a medium bowl. In a glass measuring cup, stir together the milk, cherry juice, almond extract, and vanilla. In a large bowl, beat the sugar and butter together with an electric mixer set on high speed until pale, about 3 minutes. With the mixer on low speed, add the flour mixture in thirds, alternating with the milk mixture in 2 equal additions, beating until smooth, and scraping down the sides of the bowl as needed. Fold in the cherries.

3. Using clean beaters, in a medium bowl, whip the egg whites until soft peaks form. Stir about one-quarter of the whites into the batter to loosen it, then fold in the remaining whites. Divide the batter between the prepared pans and smooth the tops.   *(continued)*

4. Bake until a wooden toothpick inserted in the centers of the cakes comes out clean, about 40 minutes. Let cool on wire cooling racks for 10 minutes. Run a dinner knife around the insides of the pans to release the cakes, invert onto the racks, and remove the pans and paper. Turn the cakes right side up on the racks and let cool completely.

5. Place a dab of frosting on a serving plate. Place 1 cake layer, flat side up, on the plate. Using a metal icing spatula, spread it with about 1 cup of the frosting. Place the second cake layer, flat side down, on top. Frost the top and sides of the cake with the remaining frosting. Arrange the cherries around the top perimeter of the cake. Let stand until the icing sets. (The cake is best the day it is made as the surface of the frosting can get crusty as it stands.)

vanilla-bean chiffon cake

Makes 16 servings

This is a masterpiece of a cake. Tall and stately, it is a blank slate for baking creativity. The extra egg whites give the cake a light, almost angel-food-like, texture. Try to use the vanilla bean paste so you get flecks of vanilla throughout the cake. It isn't a layer cake, but this beauty doesn't need much to accent its regal simplicity. You could serve it with macerated fresh fruit, as the juices are divine soaked into the cake.

2 cups plus 2 tablespoons cake flour (not self-rising), preferably unbleached

1½ cups sugar

2 teaspoons baking powder

¾ teaspoon salt

7 large eggs, separated, plus 2 large egg whites, at room temperature

¾ cup milk

½ cup vegetable oil

1 tablespoon vanilla bean paste (available at specialty grocers or online) or pure vanilla extract

¾ teaspoon cream of tartar

1. Position an oven rack in the center of the oven and preheat the oven to 325°F. Have ready a 10-inch plain tube pan (such as an angel food cake pan). Do not use a nonstick pan and do not butter or flour the pan—the batter won't rise on a slick surface.

2. Sift together the cake flour, 1¼ cups of the sugar, the baking powder, and salt into a medium bowl. In a large bowl, with an electric mixer set on high speed, beat the 7 egg yolks just until thickened. With the mixer running on high speed, add the milk, vegetable oil, and vanilla paste. With the mixer on low speed, gradually beat in the flour mixture and continue beating, scraping down the sides of the bowl with a rubber spatula as needed, for 3 minutes (set a timer).

3. In another large bowl, using clean beaters, beat the 9 egg whites with the cream of tartar until foamy. Gradually beat in the remaining ¼ cup sugar and continue beating until the mixture forms stiff, shiny peaks.

4. Gently fold the whites into the batter in 4 additions, taking care to keep the whites as fluffy as possible—this is the key to this cake's success. You don't want to deflate them. Spread the batter evenly in the pan.

5. Bake until a long bamboo skewer inserted in the center of the cake comes out clean, about 1¼ hours. Invert the pan onto the neck of a wine bottle or any tall bottle with a slender neck. (If your tube pan has a long center tube that will lift the cake above the counter surface, simply invert the pan onto the counter.) Let the cake cool completely upside down in the pan.

6. Run a dinner knife or a thin metal spatula around the inside of the pan and the tube. Push the cake up from the bottom to release it. Gently pull the bottom of the cake away from the pan bottom, and set the cake right side up on a serving plate. (The cake can be wrapped in plastic wrap and stored at room temperature for up to 3 days.)

white cake with strawberry whipped cream

Makes 12 to 16 servings

Without a single egg yolk in the batter, white cake has a pristine color. Every bakery has a recipe for white cake because its dense, moist texture makes it perfect for wedding cakes, and its neutral flavor takes well to added flavorings. For a citrus white cake, add the grated zest of 1 orange or lemon to the batter; for an almond cake, replace ½ teaspoon of the vanilla with almond extract.

Cake

Softened butter and all-purpose flour
  for the pans

3 cups cake flour (not self-rising),
  preferably unbleached

1 tablespoon baking powder

½ teaspoon salt

1 cup milk

1 tablespoon pure vanilla extract

2 cups sugar

½ pound (2 sticks) salted butter,
  at room temperature

5 large egg whites, at room temperature

¼ teaspoon cream of tartar

Frosting

1½ cups heavy cream

¾ cup strawberry jam

1. Position an oven rack in the center of the oven and preheat the oven to 350°F. Lightly butter two 9-by-2-inch round cake pans and line the bottoms with waxed or parchment paper. Dust the insides with flour and tap out the excess.

2. To make the cake: Sift the flour, baking powder, and salt into a medium bowl. In a glass measuring cup, stir together the milk and vanilla. In a large bowl, beat the sugar and butter with an electric mixer set on high speed until light and fluffy, about 3 minutes. With the mixer on low speed, in thirds beat in the flour mixture, alternating with the milk mixture in 2 equal additions, and beat until smooth, scraping down the sides of the bowl as needed.

3. In another large bowl, using clean beaters, beat the egg whites with the cream of tartar on high speed just until they form stiff, but not dry, peaks. Stir about one-third of the beaten whites into the batter to lighten it, then fold in the remaining whites. Divide the batter between the prepared pans and smooth the tops.

4. Bake until a wooden toothpick inserted in the centers of the cakes comes out clean, 30 to 35 minutes. Let cool on wire cooling racks for 10 minutes. Run a dinner knife around the insides of the pans to release the cakes. Invert onto the racks, and remove the pans and paper. Turn the cakes right side up on the racks and let cool completely.

5. To make the frosting: In a medium bowl, whip the heavy cream with an electric mixer set on high speed just until it forms soft peaks. Add ¼ cup of the jam and whip until the cream is stiff.

6. Place 1 cake layer, flat side up, on a serving plate. Using a metal icing spatula, spread it with the remaining ½ cup jam. Place the second cake layer, flat side down, on top. Frost the top and sides of the cake with the strawberry cream. Refrigerate until serving. The cake is best served within 2 hours of frosting.

yellow cake with chocolate fudge icing

Makes 12 to 16 servings

Yellow cake is enormously popular, so every baker needs a perfect recipe to bake for birthdays and other celebrations. It is about as all-American as a cake can get, and one bite is a trip down memory lane. Try this with the Chocolate Fudge Icing on page 198, which was always my grandmother's favorite.

Cake

Softened butter and all-purpose flour for the pans

2½ cups cake flour (not self-rising), preferably unbleached

1 teaspoon baking powder

1 teaspoon salt

½ teaspoon baking soda

1 cup buttermilk

1 tablespoon pure vanilla extract

2 cups sugar

½ pound (2 sticks) salted butter, at room temperature

3 large eggs plus 3 large egg yolks, at room temperature

Chocolate Fudge Icing (page 198)

1. Position a rack in the center of the oven and preheat the oven to 350°F. Butter two 9-by-2-inch round cake pans and line the bottoms with waxed or parchment paper. Dust the insides with flour and tap out the excess.

2. To make the cake, sift the flour, baking powder, salt, and baking soda into a medium bowl. In a glass measuring cup, stir together the buttermilk and vanilla. In a large bowl, beat the sugar and butter with an electric mixer set on high speed until light and fluffy, about 3 minutes. One at a time, beat in the eggs and yolks, scraping down the sides of the bowl as needed. With the mixer on low speed, in thirds beat in the flour mixture, alternating with the buttermilk mixture in 2 equal additions, and beat until smooth, scraping down the sides of the bowl as needed. Divide the batter between the prepared pans and smooth the tops.

3. Bake until a wooden toothpick inserted in the centers of the cakes comes out clean, 30 to 35 minutes. Let cool on wire cooling racks for 10 minutes. Run a dinner knife around the insides of the pans to release the cakes, invert onto the racks, and remove the pans and paper. Turn the cakes right side up on the racks and let cool completely.

4. Place a dab of icing on a serving plate. Place 1 cake layer, flat side up, on the plate. Spread it with 1 cup of icing. Place the second cake layer, flat side down, on top. Frost the top and sides of the cake with the remaining icing.

hazelnut cake with nutella cream

Makes 12 to 16 servings

This dense, moist layer cake has more of a sophisticated European feeling than most of my desserts, which tend to remind me of the kind of homespun baking that I grew up with. The butter in the cake layers will make them very firm if refrigerated, so it is best to serve the cake within an hour or so of frosting it with the whipped cream.

Cake

Softened butter and all-purpose flour
  for the pans

2 cups cake flour (not self-rising),
  preferably unbleached

1½ cups hazelnut flour or finely ground
  hazelnuts (see Note)

1½ teaspoons baking powder

¼ teaspoon baking soda

⅛ teaspoon salt

1 cup buttermilk

2 tablespoons hazelnut liqueur

12 tablespoons (1½ sticks) salted butter,
  at room temperature

1 cup firmly packed dark brown sugar

¼ cup granulated sugar

3 tablespoons praline paste
  (see Note, page 90)

3 large eggs plus 2 large egg yolks,
  at room temperature

Nutella Whipped Cream (page 201)

1. Position an oven rack in the center of the oven and preheat the oven to 350°F. Lightly butter two 9-by-2-inch round cake pans and line the bottoms with waxed or parchment paper. Dust the insides with flour and tap out the excess.

2. To make the cake: In a medium bowl, whisk together the flour, hazelnut flour, baking powder, baking soda, and salt. In a glass measuring cup, stir together the buttermilk and liqueur. In a large bowl, beat the butter with an electric mixer set on high speed until creamy, about 1 minute. Gradually beat in the brown and granulated sugars and continue beating until light and fluffy, about 2 minutes. Beat in the praline paste. One at a time, beat in the eggs and yolks, scraping down the sides of the bowl as needed. With the mixer on low speed, beat in the flour mixture in thirds, alternating with the buttermilk mixture in 2 equal additions, beating until smooth and scraping down the sides of the bowl as needed. Divide the batter between the prepared pans and smooth the tops.   *(continued)*

3. Bake until a wooden toothpick inserted in the centers of the cakes comes out clean, about 30 minutes. Let cool on wire cooling racks for 10 minutes. Run a dinner knife around the insides of the pans to release the cakes, invert onto the racks, and remove the pans and paper. Turn the cakes right side up on the racks and let cool completely.

4. Place 1 cake layer, flat side up, on a serving plate. Using a metal icing spatula, spread it with about 1 cup of the whipped cream. Place the second cake layer, flat side down, on top. Frost the top and sides of the cake with the remaining whipped cream. (Refrigerate until serving, but the cake is best served within 2 hours of frosting.)

Note: Hazelnut flour is available at natural food stores and many supermarkets. To grind hazelnuts at home, toast and skin 1⅔ cups hazelnuts (see page 17). Pulse in a food processor until coarsely chopped. Add ½ cup of the cake flour from the recipe and pulse until the hazelnuts are very finely chopped. Add this mixture, along with the remaining cake flour, as directed in the recipe.

date-banana cake with cream cheese icing

Makes 12 to 16 servings

When I was at SUNY Cobleskill, my favorite baking professor, Robert Sielaff, gave me this delicious recipe with sweet bananas, chewy dates, and crunchy walnuts in every bite. The frosted cake keeps for several days. If you like, 3 cups of Whipped Cream (see page 200) makes a good substitute for the cream cheese icing. In that case, refrigerate the plastic-wrapped layers for up to 3 days, and then frost with the whipped cream just before serving.

Cake

1½ cups old-fashioned (rolled) oats

1½ cups boiling water

Softened butter and all-purpose flour for the pans

1½ cups unbleached all-purpose flour

¾ teaspoon ground cloves

¾ teaspoon salt

¾ teaspoon baking powder

½ teaspoon baking soda

½ teaspoon ground cinnamon

1½ cups firmly packed dark brown sugar

¾ cup granulated sugar

12 tablespoons (1½ sticks) salted butter, at room temperature

3 large eggs, at room temperature

¾ cup mashed fully ripe bananas (about 1½ large bananas)

¾ cup pitted and chopped (¼-inch) dates

¾ cup coarsely chopped walnuts

Cream Cheese Icing (page 197)

1. In a heatproof bowl, combine the oats and boiling water. Let cool.

2. Position an oven rack in the center of the oven and preheat the oven to 350°F. Lightly butter two 9-by-2-inch round cake pans and line the bottoms with waxed or parchment paper. Dust the insides with flour and tap out the excess.

3. To make the cake: In a medium bowl, whisk together the flour, cloves, salt, baking powder, baking soda, and cinnamon. In a large bowl, beat the brown sugar, granulated sugar, and butter together with an electric mixer set on high speed until light and fluffy, about 3 minutes. One at a time, beat in the eggs, scraping down the sides of the bowl as needed. With the mixer on low speed, add the flour mixture in thirds, beating until smooth, and scraping down the sides of the bowl as needed. Beat in the mashed bananas. Fold in the dates and walnuts. Divide the batter between the prepared pans and smooth the tops.

4. Bake until a wooden toothpick inserted in the centers of the cakes comes out clean, about 40 minutes. Let cool on wire cooling racks for 10 minutes. Run a dinner knife around the insides of the pans to release the cakes, invert onto the racks, and remove the pans and paper. Turn the cakes right side up on the racks and let cool completely.

5. Place a dab of icing on a serving plate. Place 1 cake layer, flat side up, on the plate. Using a metal icing spatula, spread it with about 1 cup of the icing. Place the second cake layer, flat side down, on top. Frost the top and sides of the cake with the remaining icing. (The cake can be refrigerated for up to 3 days. Let stand at room temperature for 2 hours before serving.)

cardamom cake (kardemummakaka)

Makes 8 servings

Cardamom is a wild card in baking—too much, and it is too strong, but ground cardamom can be flavorless, probably because it is stale. I got this authentic Swedish cardamom cake from my customer Ken (whose surname I never learned), who got it from his sister-in-law, Irene Johansen. It is light and not too sweet. Be sure to use freshly ground cardamom seeds, ground in a clean coffee grinder or with a mortar and pestle.

Cake
Softened butter for the pan
2⅓ cups unbleached all-purpose flour
1 tablespoon baking powder
1½ teaspoon freshly ground cardamom
¼ teaspoon salt
1 cup plus 2 tablespoons sugar
3 large eggs, at room temperature

12 tablespoons (1½ sticks) salted butter, melted and cooled until tepid
1 teaspoon pure vanilla extract
1 cup milk
⅔ cup natural or blanched sliced almonds

Whipped Cream (page 200) for serving
Fresh seasonal fruit (berries are nice) for serving

1. Position an oven rack in the center of the oven and preheat the oven to 350°F. Butter a 9-by-3-inch springform pan.

2. To make the cake: In a medium bowl, whisk together the flour, baking powder, cardamom, and salt. In a large bowl, whip 1 cup of the sugar and the eggs with an electric mixer set on high speed until pale yellow and fluffy, about 5 minutes (less time if you are using a heavy-duty standing mixer with a whisk attachment). With the mixer running, drizzle in the tepid melted butter and the vanilla. Scrape down the sides of the bowl. With the mixer on low speed, beat in the flour mixture in thirds, alternating with the milk in 2 equal additions, scraping down the sides of the bowl as needed. Spread the batter evenly in the prepared pan. Sprinkle the almonds evenly over the top of the batter, followed by the remaining 2 tablespoons sugar. Put the pan on a rimmed baking sheet.

3. Bake until a wooden toothpick inserted in the center of the cake comes out clean, about 45 minutes. Let cool on a wire cooling rack for 15 minutes. Remove the sides of the pan, invert the cake onto the rack, and remove the pan bottom. Turn the cake right side up on the rack and let cool completely.

4. Slice the cake and serve with the whipped cream and fruit.

beet and rhubarb cake with ginger icing

Makes 12 servings

When my niece Julia King made a spectacular beet and rhubarb soup for Easter dinner, it inspired me to make this dessert, which is not too far removed from carrot cake. The batter goes into the oven a dark mauve but bakes into the familiar "golden brown."

Cake

Softened butter and all-purpose flour
  for the pans

2 cups unbleached all-purpose flour

2 teaspoons ground cinnamon

1 teaspoon baking powder

1 teaspoon baking soda

½ teaspoon salt

1¼ cups sugar

1 cup olive oil (not extra virgin)

4 large eggs, at room temperature

1 teaspoon pure vanilla extract

4 medium beets, peeled and shredded
  (2 cups)

1½ cups diced (¼-inch) rhubarb

1 cup unsweetened coconut flakes
  (not desiccated), available at natural
  food stores and online

Ginger Cream Cheese Icing (page 197)

1. Position an oven rack in the center of the oven and preheat the oven to 325°F. Lightly butter two 8-by-2-inch round cake pans and line the bottoms with waxed or parchment paper. Dust the insides with flour and tap out the excess.

2. To make the cake: In a medium bowl, whisk together the flour, cinnamon, baking powder, baking soda, and salt. In a large bowl, beat the sugar and oil with an electric mixer set on high speed until pale, about 2 minutes. One at a time, beat in the eggs, beating well after each addition. Beat in the vanilla. With the mixer on low speed, add the flour mixture in thirds, scraping down the sides of the bowl as needed. Stir in the beets, rhubarb, and coconut. Divide the batter between the prepared pans and smooth the tops.

3. Bake until the cakes spring back when pressed in the center with your fingertip, 40 to 45 minutes. Let cool on wire cooling racks for 10 minutes. Run a dinner knife around the insides of the pans to release the cakes, invert onto the racks, and remove the pans and paper. Turn right side up on the racks and let cool completely.

4. Place a dab of icing on a serving plate. Place 1 cake layer, flat side up, on the plate. Using a metal icing spatula, spread it with about 1 cup of the icing. Place the second cake layer, flat side down, on top. Frost the top and sides of the cake with the remaining icing. (The cake can be refrigerated for 1 day.) Serve chilled or at room temperature.

chocolate chip layer cake for marco

Makes 12 to 16 servings

Marco Ochoa has worked at Tate's for many years, and I developed this cake with the beloved flavors of a chocolate chip cookie for him. If you don't have two 9-by-3 pans, use three 8-by-1½-inch pans and make cupcakes with the excess batter. Regular chips are too large for the cake, so be sure to use miniature chips. Enjoy a slice with a scoop of coffee ice cream.

Cake
Softened butter and all-purpose flour
   for the pans
3½ cups unbleached all-purpose flour
2 teaspoons baking powder
1 teaspoon baking soda
1 teaspoon salt
2 cups buttermilk
1 tablespoon pure vanilla extract

2 cups firmly packed dark brown sugar
½ pound (2 sticks) salted butter,
   at room temperature
2 large eggs plus 2 large egg yolks,
   at room temperature
1½ cups (9 ounces) miniature chocolate chips

Milk Chocolate Mocha Frosting (page 199)

1. Position an oven rack in the center of the oven and preheat the oven to 350°F. Lightly butter two 9-by-3-inch round cake pans (springform pans are fine) and line the bottoms with waxed or parchment paper. Dust the insides with flour and tap out the excess.

2. To make the cake: In a medium bowl, whisk together the flour, baking powder, baking soda, and salt. In a glass measuring cup, mix together the buttermilk and vanilla. In a large bowl, beat the brown sugar and butter together with an electric mixer set on high speed until light and fluffy, about 3 minutes. One at a time, beat in the eggs and yolks, beating well after each addition. With the mixer on low speed, add the flour mixture in thirds, alternating with the buttermilk mixture in 2 equal additions, beating until smooth, and scraping down the sides of the bowl as needed. Fold in the chocolate chips. Divide the batter between the prepared pans and smooth the tops.

3. Bake until a wooden toothpick in the centers of the cakes comes out clean, about 40 minutes. Let cool on wire cooling racks for 10 minutes. Run a dinner knife around the insides of the pans to release the cakes, invert onto the racks, and remove the pans and paper. Turn the cakes right side up on the racks and let cool completely. *(continued)*

4. Place a dab of frosting on a serving plate. Place 1 cake layer, flat side up, on the plate. Using a metal icing spatula, spread it with 1 cup of the frosting. Place the second cake layer, flat side down, on top. Frost the top and sides of the cake with the remaining frosting. (The cake is best the day it is made.)

super-moist chocolate cake with vanilla icing

Makes 12 to 16 servings

This is a classic dark chocolate cake that every baker should have on file. (I also use it for the Blackout Cupcakes on page 169.) While there are many options for frosting (such as Nutella Whipped Cream or the Fluffy Vanilla Icing on pages 201 and 196), my very favorite is my aunt's vanilla flour icing with raspberry jam between the layers. Keep two layers in the freezer and you will always be ready to celebrate!

Cake
Softened butter and all-purpose flour
  for the pans
3 ounces unsweetened chocolate,
  chopped
2 ounces semisweet chocolate, chopped
2 cups cake flour (not self-rising),
  preferably unbleached
¼ cup natural cocoa powder
1½ teaspoons baking soda
1 teaspoon instant espresso powder
½ teaspoon salt

½ cup buttermilk
2 teaspoons pure vanilla extract
2 cups firmly packed dark brown sugar
½ pound (2 sticks) salted butter,
  at room temperature
3 large eggs plus 1 large egg yolk,
  at room temperature
1 cup boiling water

½ cup raspberry jam
Aunt Betty's Flour Icing (page 195)

1. Position an oven rack in the center of the oven and preheat the oven to 350°F. Lightly butter two 9-by-2-inch round cake pans and line the bottoms with waxed or parchment paper. Dust the insides with flour and tap out the excess.

2. To make the cake: In a microwave oven on Medium (50%), in a microwave-safe bowl, heat the chocolate, stirring at 30-second intervals, until just melted, about 2 minutes. Let cool until tepid but still fluid.

3. Sift the flour, cocoa powder, baking soda, espresso powder, and salt in a medium bowl. In a glass measuring cup, stir together the buttermilk and vanilla. In a large bowl, beat the brown sugar and butter with an electric mixer set on high speed until the mixture is pale and fluffy, about 3 minutes. One at a time, beat in the eggs and yolk, scraping down the sides of the bowl with a rubber spatula as needed. Beat in the tepid chocolate. With the machine on low speed, in thirds beat in the flour mixture, alternating with 2 equal additions of the buttermilk mixture, beating until smooth and scraping down the sides of the bowl as needed. Gradually beat in the boiling water. Divide the batter among the prepared pans and smooth the tops.

4. Bake until a wooden toothpick inserted in the center of the cakes comes out clean, 30 to 35 minutes. Let cool on wire cooling racks for 10 minutes. Run a dinner knife around the insides of the pans to release the cakes. Invert onto the racks and remove the pans and paper. Turn the cakes right side up on the racks and let cool completely.

5. Place 1 cake layer, flat side up, on the plate. Using a metal icing spatula, spread with the jam. Place the second cake layer, flat side down, on top. Frost the top and sides of the cake with the icing. (The cake can be refrigerated for up to 1 day. Let stand at room temperature for 2 hours before serving.) Slice and serve.

blackout cupcakes

Makes 15 cupcakes

I held Sunday taste tests with friends that grew up in Brooklyn in order to re-create the famous blackout cake from Ebinger's bakery. Here is the result with chocolate cake, chocolate pudding icing, and a chocolate crumb topping.

Softened butter and all-purpose flour for the pans

Batter for the Super Moist Chocolate Layer Cake (page 166)

Chocolate Pudding Icing

½ cup cornstarch

1½ cups water

1¼ cups sugar

½ cup Dutch-processed cocoa powder

2 teaspoons light corn syrup

4 tablespoons (½ stick) salted butter, at room temperature

1 teaspoon pure vanilla extract

2 ounces semisweet chocolate, finely chopped

1. Position an oven rack in the center of the oven and preheat the oven to 350°F. Line fifteen 3-by-1½-inch muffin cups with paper liners. Lightly butter a 9-by-2-inch round cake pan. Line the bottom with parchment paper or waxed paper. Dust the inside with flour and tap out the excess.

2. Using a ⅓-cup food portion scoop or a spoon, transfer the batter to the muffin cups, filling them about three-quarters full. Spread the remaining batter in the cake pan. Put the pans in the oven and bake until a wooden toothpick inserted in the center of a cupcake comes out clean, about 25 minutes. Remove the muffin pans and set on wire cooling racks. Continue baking the cake until a wooden toothpick inserted in the center comes out clean, about 5 minutes more. Set the pan on a wire cooling rack. Let cool in the pans on the racks for 10 minutes.

3. Remove the cupcakes from the pans and transfer to the racks. Run a knife around the inside of the cake pan to release the cake, invert onto a rack, and remove the pan and paper. Let the cupcakes and cake cool completely.

4. To make the icing: In a small bowl, whisk the cornstarch into ¼ cup of the water to make a smooth paste. In a medium saucepan, whisk the remaining 1¼ cups of water with the sugar, cocoa powder, and corn syrup. Bring to a boil over medium heat, stirring constantly.

(continued)

Whisk the cornstarch mixture again, and stir into the cocoa mixture. Reduce the heat to medium-low and simmer, stirring often, until the mixture is as thick as pudding and very dark brown, about 3 minutes. Remove from the heat and stir in the butter and vanilla. Add the chocolate. Let stand for 2 minutes and stir until the chocolate is melted. Pour into a small bowl and press plastic wrap directly against the surface of the chocolate mixture. Refrigerate until chilled.

5. Crumble the cake well with your hands. Put into a pie plate or shallow bowl.

6. Stir the icing well to smooth it out. Using a ⅓-cup food portion scoop, mound icing on top of each cupcake. Gently spread the icing to the edges of each cupcake to shape the icing into a dome. Roll the edges of each cupcake in the crumbs to coat, then the top. (The cupcakes can be refrigerated for up to 1 day. Let stand at room temperature for 2 hours before serving.)

milk chocolate cake

Makes 9 servings

I often melt leftover holiday milk chocolate to create this simple sheet cake with light chocolate flavor. The better the chocolate, the better the cake.

Softened butter for the pan
8 ounces milk chocolate, finely chopped
1½ cups unbleached all-purpose flour
1 cup old-fashioned (rolled) oats
2 teaspoons baking powder
½ teaspoon salt

½ cup heavy cream
1 teaspoon instant espresso powder
¾ cup firmly packed dark brown sugar
8 tablespoons (1 stick) salted butter, at room temperature
2 large eggs, at room temperature

1. Position an oven rack in the center of the oven and preheat the oven to 325°F. Lightly butter a 9-inch square baking pan.

2. Put the milk chocolate in a heatproof bowl. Bring a skillet of water to a simmer over medium heat. Remove from the heat, place the bowl in the hot water, and let stand, stirring occasionally, until the chocolate is melted; be sure not to get any water in the bowl. Remove the bowl from the water and let cool until tepid.

3. In a medium bowl, whisk together the flour, oats, baking powder, and salt. In a glass measuring cup, whisk together the heavy cream and espresso powder. In a large bowl, beat the brown sugar and butter with an electric mixer set on high speed until pale and fluffy, about 3 minutes. One at a time, beat in the eggs, scraping down the sides of the bowl as needed. Beat in the chocolate. With the mixer on low speed, beat in the flour mixture in thirds, alternating with the cream mixture in 2 equal additions, beating until smooth and scraping down the sides of the bowl as needed. Spread the batter in prepared pan.

4. Bake until a wooden toothpick inserted in the center of the cake comes out clean, about 40 minutes. (For a moister, more brownie-like cake, bake only until the toothpick comes out with moist crumbs, 30 to 35 minutes.) Let cool completely in the pan on a wire cooling rack.

white chocolate cupcakes
with raspberry filling

Makes 12 cupcakes

By itself, white chocolate is not a favorite of mine, but it works very well to add vanilla flavor to these cupcakes. A tart jam filling contrasts with the sweetness of the cupcakes and frosting; I like raspberry, though strawberry or even currant are also good. The cupcakes are just fine without the filling, too. If you'd like to make this as a layer cake, double the recipe, use two 9-inch pans, and bake for about 40 minutes.

Cupcakes

5 ounces white chocolate, finely chopped

1¼ cups unbleached all-purpose flour

¼ cup cake flour (not self-rising), preferably unbleached

1 teaspoon baking powder

½ teaspoon salt

1 cup milk

1 tablespoon pure vanilla extract

⅔ cup sugar

4 tablespoons (½ stick) salted butter, at room temperature

2 large eggs, at room temperature

Assembly

¾ cup raspberry jam

White Chocolate Cream Cheese Icing (page 197)

(continued)

1. To make the cupcakes: Put the white chocolate in a heatproof bowl. Bring a skillet of water to a simmer over medium heat. Remove from the heat, place the bowl in the hot water, and let stand, stirring occasionally, until the white chocolate is melted; be sure not to get any water in the bowl. Remove the bowl from the water and let cool until tepid.

2. Position a rack in the center of the oven and preheat the oven to 350°F. Line twelve 3-by-1½-inch muffin cups with paper liners.

3. In a small bowl, whisk together the flour, cake flour, baking powder, and salt. In a glass measuring cup, stir together the milk and vanilla. In a large bowl, beat the sugar and butter with an electric mixer set on high speed until light and fluffy, about 3 minutes. One at a time, beat in the eggs, scraping down the sides of the bowl as needed. Beat in the tepid white chocolate. With the mixer on low speed, in thirds beat in the flour mixture, alternating with the milk mixture in 2 equal additions, and beat until smooth, scraping down the sides of the bowl as needed. Using a ⅓-cup food portion scoop or a spoon, transfer the batter into the prepared cups; they will be full.

4. Bake until a wooden toothpick inserted the center of a cupcake comes out clean, 25 to 30 minutes. These will not rise or turn golden brown like other cakes; do not overbake. Let the cupcakes cool in the pan for 10 to 15 minutes. Remove the cupcakes from the pan and let cool completely on a wire cooling rack.

5. Put the jam in a pastry bag fitted with a plain tip about ½ inch wide. Insert the tip about ½ inch deep into a cupcake and squeeze to pipe about a tablespoon of jam into it. Repeat with the remaining cupcakes and jam. Frost the tops of the cupcakes with the icing. (For an especially professional look, use an ice-cream scoop to top each cupcake with the icing, then use a small icing spatula to smooth each portion of icing into a dome.)

6. Refrigerate until serving. Remove from the refrigerator at least 1 hour before serving.

chapter 6

health & lifestyle
baked goods

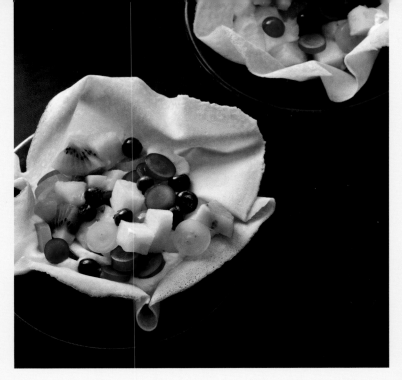

TIPS FOR HEALTH AND LIFESTYLE BAKED GOODS

✳ The most common ingredients in whole-grain cooking—flours, meals, nuts, and seeds—contain oils that can go rancid fairly quickly, so store them in zip-tight plastic bags so they don't pick up any unwanted flavors, in the refrigerator or freezer. Let them stand at room temperature for an hour or so before using to lose their chill.

✳ Stir whole-grain batters and doughs with a light hand to keep the air bubbles intact.

✳ Flaxseed is an excellent source of omega-3 fatty acids, which have been shown to have many health benefits. The seeds are quite hard, and often ground before use. Preground flaxseed is sold as flaxseed meal, or grind the seeds at home in a blender or coffee grinder. (Clean the coffee grinder before and after by processing raw rice until it is powdered; discard the ground rice.)

banana flaxseed muffins

Makes 12 muffins

A few years ago, I introduced this low-fat whole-grain banana muffin in early January as an antidote to the annual holiday season excess. It was so popular that it remained on the menu and has become one of Tate's signature items. You can use any of the whole wheat flours listed, but the pastry flour makes a slightly lighter muffin. Bake a dozen, individually wrap, and freeze to have ready for your morning coffee or tea or as an afternoon snack.

Nonstick oil spray (optional)

1½ cups whole wheat flour, white whole wheat flour, or whole wheat pastry flour

½ cup chopped pecans

¼ cup ground flaxseed (flaxseed meal)

2 teaspoons baking powder

1 teaspoon baking soda

½ teaspoon ground cinnamon

¼ teaspoon salt

1 cup mashed fully ripe bananas (2 large bananas)

¾ cup low-fat or nonfat yogurt

¼ cup plus 2 tablespoons sugar

2 tablespoons walnut oil, canola oil, or salted butter, melted

1 large egg or 2 large egg whites, at room temperature

1 teaspoon pure vanilla extract

2 tablespoons old-fashioned (rolled) oats for sprinkling (optional)

1. Position a rack in the center of the oven and preheat the oven to 375°F. Spray twelve 3-by-1½-inch muffin cups with oil or line them with paper liners.

2. In a large bowl, whisk together the whole wheat flour, pecans, ground flaxseed, baking powder, baking soda, cinnamon, and salt. In another bowl, whisk together the mashed bananas, yogurt, sugar, walnut oil, egg, and vanilla. Pour into the flour mixture and fold in with a rubber spatula just until combined. Do not overmix.

3. Using a ⅓-cup food portion scoop or a spoon, transfer the batter to the prepared muffin cups. The cups will be fairly full. Sprinkle the tops with the oats, if using.

4. Bake until a muffin springs back when pressed on the top with your fingertip, 20 to 25 minutes. Let the muffins cool in the pan on a wire cooling rack for 5 minutes. Remove the muffins from the pan and let cool completely on the rack.

vegan blueberry lemon scuffins

Makes 6 scuffins

Alyssa Marie came to my family's farm as a member of the World Wide Opportunities on Organic Farms. A delightful young woman, she loves baking, and she taught me a few things about vegan cooking. These pastries, Alyssa's cross between a muffin and a scone with a thick berry glaze, even ended up being sold at the family farm stand! Check out her blog at www.alyssamariepatisserie.blogspot.com

Scuffins

2½ cups unbleached all-purpose flour

⅓ cup sugar

1 tablespoon baking powder

¼ teaspoon salt

8 tablespoons (1 stick) cold vegan soy margarine, cut into ½-inch cubes

½ cup water or almond milk

¼ cup fresh lemon juice

Grated zest of 1 lemon

1 cup fresh or frozen (not thawed) blueberries

Blueberry Rosemary Glaze

⅔ cup fresh or thawed frozen blueberries

Leaves from one 3-inch sprig fresh rosemary

½ cup confectioners' sugar

2 tablespoons fresh lemon juice

2 teaspoons pure vanilla extract

⅛ teaspoon cornstarch

1. To make the scuffins: In a large bowl, whisk together the flour, sugar, baking powder, and salt. Using a pastry blender, cut in the margarine until the mixture is crumbly with some pea-sized pieces of margarine. In a small bowl, whisk together the water, lemon juice, and lemon zest. Freeze the flour and water mixtures in their separate bowls for 15 minutes.

2. Meanwhile, position an oven rack in the center of the oven and preheat the oven to 425°F. Line a large rimmed baking sheet with parchment paper or a silicone baking mat.

3. Add the blueberries to the flour mixture and toss to coat. Stir in the water mixture. The dough will seem dry. Turn it out onto a work surface and knead gently until it comes together. Do not overwork. Pat into a 1-inch-thick disk. Cut into 6 wedges, like a pizza. Place the wedges 4 inches apart on the prepared baking sheet.

4. Bake until golden brown, about 30 minutes. Let cool on the pan for 10 minutes.

(continued)

5. Meanwhile, make the glaze: In a food processor, puree the blueberries, rosemary, confectioners' sugar, lemon juice, vanilla, and cornstarch. Transfer to a small saucepan and bring to a boil, stirring often, over medium heat. Cook, stirring often, until slightly thickened, about 30 seconds. Remove from the heat and let cool.

6. Transfer the warm scuffins to a wire cooling rack set over a rimmed baking sheet. Spoon and spread the glaze over the scuffins. Let cool completely.

white whole wheat blueberry muffins

Makes 12 muffins

My friend Anne Rachel loves this muffin, which has a lot of added nutritional value with white whole wheat flour and flax meal. We walk on the beach a few times a week, and one time, I lost my keys in the sand. We tried to find them, retracing our hour-long walk, but we had no luck. Anne was kind enough to drive me home for my spare set, and on our next walk, I surprised her with these muffins, still warm from the oven.

Softened butter for the pan

3 cups white whole wheat flour

¼ cup ground flaxseed (flaxseed meal)

½ cup sugar

1½ tablespoons baking powder

½ teaspoon salt

1¼ cups low-fat milk

8 tablespoons (1 stick) salted butter, melted

½ cup unsweetened applesauce

2 large eggs, at room temperature

2 cups fresh or frozen (not thawed) blueberries

1. Position an oven rack in the center of the oven and preheat the oven to 400°F. Butter twelve 3-by-1½-inch muffin cups.

2. In a large bowl, whisk together the flour, ground flaxseed, sugar, baking powder, and salt. In a separate bowl, whisk together the milk, melted butter, applesauce, and eggs. Pour into the flour mixture and stir just until combined. Fold in the blueberries. Spoon the batter into the prepared muffin cups. The cups will be very full, but they won't overflow during baking.

3. Bake until a wooden toothpick inserted in center of a muffin comes out clean, 25 to 30 minutes. Let the muffins cool in the pan on a wire cooling rack for 10 to 15 minutes. Remove the muffins from the pan and let cool completely on the rack.

lemon cream pie in meringue crust

Makes 8 servings

My sister, Karin Driscoll, gave me the recipe for this pie years ago, and it is still a favorite. It consists of sweet crunchy meringue, a lemony filling, and whipped cream, all heavenly to eat by themselves, but when combined...! Note that the pie must chill for a day before serving, a step that makes the meringue crust delectably chewy.

Meringue Crust
Softened butter for the pie plate
4 large egg whites, at room temperature
¼ teaspoon cream of tartar
¾ cup sugar

Filling
⅓ cup fresh lemon juice
5 large egg yolks
¼ cup plus 3 tablespoons sugar
2 tablespoons salted butter
Grated zest of 1 lemon
1½ cups heavy cream
1 teaspoon pure vanilla extract

1. Make the pie the day before serving. Position an oven rack in the center of the oven and preheat the oven to 275°F. Lightly butter a 9-inch pie plate.

2. To make the crust: In a large bowl, beat the egg whites with an electric mixer set on high speed until frothy. Add the cream of tartar and beat just until stiff peaks form. Gradually beat in the sugar and beat until the peaks are very stiff and shiny. Spoon the meringue into the prepared pie plate, shaping it into a thick pie shell with the back of the spoon. (The meringue shell will bake exactly as shaped, so make it deep enough to hold the filling.) Bake until the meringue is firm and golden brown, about 1 hour. Let cool on a wire cooling rack.

3. To prepare the lemon filling: In the top of a double boiler, whisk together the lemon juice, yolks, ¼ cup of the sugar, and butter. Heat over simmering water, stirring constantly with a wooden spoon, until an instant-read thermometer inserted in the mixture reads 185°F, about 3 minutes. (Or if you run your finger through the mixture on the spoon, it should cut a swath.) Strain the lemon mixture through a wire sieve into a heatproof bowl to remove any bits of egg. Stir in the lemon zest. Cover with plastic wrap and let the lemon mixture cool completely.

(continued)

4. In a separate bowl, whip the cream with the remaining 3 tablespoons sugar and the vanilla until stiff peaks form. Spread half of the whipped cream in the meringue shell. Gently spread the lemon mixture over it, then pile the remaining cream on top. Refrigerate for at least 12 hours and up to 24 hours.

5. Cut into wedges and serve chilled.

heart-healthy chocolate pie

Makes 8 servings

I entered this dense, creamy, and rich chocolate pie in our local American Heart Association Heart-Healthy Bake-Off. With stiff competition from six other professional bakers, I was surprised to win. Regardless of its healthful profile, this pie is a great addition to your dessert repertoire. To reduce calories and fat further, serve it without the creamy topping.

Low-Fat Graham Cracker Crust

2 cups low-fat graham cracker crumbs (from about 2 sleeves of crackers, crushed in the food processor)

2 tablespoons almond butter

4 tablespoons (½ stick) unsalted butter, melted

2 tablespoons Grade B pure maple syrup

Filling

6 ounces semisweet chocolate, finely chopped

8 ounces low-fat cream cheese, at room temperature

3 tablespoons dark brown sugar

8 ounces silken tofu, drained

2 teaspoons pure vanilla extract

2 large egg whites, at room temperature

Topping

½ cup heavy cream

½ cup plain nonfat Greek yogurt

⅓ cup fruit-sweetened seedless raspberry spread

2 tablespoons granulated sugar (optional)

1 teaspoon pure vanilla extract

Raspberry Coulis (page 201)

Two 6-ounce baskets fresh raspberries

1. Position an oven rack in the center of the oven and preheat the oven to 325°F.

2. To make the crust: Pulse the graham cracker crumbs, almond butter, melted butter, and maple syrup together in a food processor until the crumbs are evenly moistened. Press evenly onto the bottom and sides of a 9-inch pie plate. Do not press too hard, or the crust will be tough. Refrigerate.

3. To make the filling: Heat the chocolate in a microwave-safe bowl at Medium (50% power), stirring at 30-second intervals, until melted and smooth, about 2 minutes. Let cool until tepid but fluid.

4. In a large bowl, beat the cream cheese and brown sugar with an electric mixer set on high speed until creamy, about 1 minute, scraping down the sides of the bowl as needed. Add the tofu and vanilla and beat until the tofu is smooth. Add the melted chocolate and beat until combined, scraping down the bowl as needed.

5. In a medium bowl, using clean beaters, beat the egg whites on high speed until they form stiff, but not dry, peaks. Stir about one-quarter of the whites into the chocolate mixture to lighten it, then fold in the remaining whites. Spread evenly in the prepared crust. Place on a rimmed baking sheet.

6. Bake until the filling looks set but still has a wet area in the center, about 40 minutes. Do not overbake. Let cool completely on a wire cooling rack. Refrigerate until chilled, at least 2 hours, or up to 1 day.

7. Just before serving, make the topping: Whip the cream with an electric mixer on high speed until it begins to thicken. Add the yogurt, raspberry spread, sugar, if using, and vanilla and continue whipping until the mixture forms stiff peaks. Spread on top of the pie filling. Slice and serve chilled, with the raspberry coulis and fresh raspberries.

vegan sweet potato pie

Makes 8 servings

Every Thanksgiving menu needs a pie that features the flavors of fall. Sweet potato pie is a nice alternative to the familiar pumpkin. Like its cousin, it is creamy, smooth, and not too sweet with wonderful warm spices, but this one gets a deep flavor from dried fruits. And it is not baked, which is a plus when the ovens are filled with other food for the feast.

Nut Crust

1 cup pecan pieces

1 cup whole natural almonds

⅓ cup pitted and coarsely chopped dates

Filling

1 cup canned coconut milk (shake well before measuring)

½ cup Grade B pure maple syrup

½ cup dried currants or raisins

¼ cup pitted and coarsely chopped dates

¼ cup pitted and coarsely chopped prunes (dried plums)

¼ cup fresh orange juice

1 tablespoon flaked agar-agar

1 teaspoon well-crushed kuzu root starch

1 tablespoon pure vanilla extract

1 pound silken tofu, drained

1 cup baked, peeled, and mashed sweet potato or orange-fleshed yam (see page 53)

1 teaspoon ground cinnamon

1 teaspoon ground ginger

¼ teaspoon freshly grated nutmeg

Grated zest of 1 orange or lemon

1. To make the nut crust: In a food processor, process the pecans, almonds, and dates until the nuts are finely ground and the mixture forms a thick paste. Press firmly and evenly into the bottom and sides of a 9-by-2-inch deep-dish pie plate.

2. To make the filling: In a small saucepan, bring the coconut milk, maple syrup, currants, dates, prunes, orange juice, agar-agar, and kuzu root starch to a simmer over medium heat, stirring often. Reduce the heat to medium-low and simmer, stirring often, until the fruit softens, about 10 minutes. Remove from the heat and stir in the vanilla.

3. In the food processor, process the tofu, sweet potato, cinnamon, ginger, nutmeg, and orange zest until smooth. Add the hot fruit mixture and puree. Pour into the nut crust and let cool to room temperature.

4. Cover the pie with plastic wrap and refrigerate until the filling is firm, at least 3 hours, or up to 1 day. Slice and serve chilled.

gluten-free spice cake

Makes 6 to 8 servings

Here's another wonderful recipe from Robin King. You'll find 6-inch pans at shops and online stores that cater to cake bakers.

Spice Cake
Nonstick oil spray for the pans
1⅓ cups oat flour
⅔ cup almond milk
½ cup granulated sugar
½ cup firmly packed dark brown sugar
3 large eggs, at room temperature
⅓ cup unsweetened applesauce
¼ cup walnut oil
2 teaspoons fresh lemon juice
2 teaspoons baking powder
1 teaspoon baking soda
1 teaspoon pure vanilla extract

1 teaspoon ground cinnamon
1 teaspoon xanthan gum
    (available at natural food stores,
    online, and many supermarkets)
½ teaspoon ground allspice
½ teaspoon freshly grated nutmeg
½ teaspoon salt

Frosting
1⅓ cups heavy cream
¼ cup Grade B pure maple syrup
¼ teaspoon maple extract
1 cup toasted and coarsely chopped pecans

1. Position an oven rack in the center of the oven and preheat the oven to 350°F. Spray two 6-by-2-inch round cake pans with oil. Line the bottoms with rounds of parchment or waxed paper and spray the paper.

2. To make the cake: In a large bowl, using a wooden spoon, stir all of the ingredients together make a thin batter. Divide evenly between the prepared pans.

3. Bake until the cakes spring back when pressed in the center with a fingertip, about 40 minutes. Let cool in the pans on a wire cooling rack for 10 minutes. Run a dinner knife around the insides of the pans to loosen the cakes. Invert the cakes onto wire cooling racks, and unmold. Remove the paper, turn the cakes right side up on the rack, and let cool completely.

4. To make the frosting: In a medium bowl, whip the cream, maple syrup and extract with an electric mixer set on high speed until stiff peaks form. Place 1 cake layer, flat side up, on a serving plate. Spread with about ½ cup of the whipped cream. Top with the second layer cake, flat side down. Frost the top and sides of the cake with the remaining cream. Press the pecans onto the top and sides of the cake. Refrigerate until ready to serve.

da bonac bowl

Makes 1 serving

East Hampton High School students Peter Shilowich, Nicholas Quiroz, Jen Gomez, Brianna Loffreno, and Luisa Torres created this prize-winning recipe for the Long Island Family & Consumer Sciences Healthy Snack Challenge. The challenge was to design a quickly prepared nutritional snack that was 200 calories or less. A beautiful fruit salad for one in a crepe bowl, it is named after the school's football team, The Bonackers. Clever kids!

Nonstick oil spray

One 9-inch store-bought crepe, such as Melissa's (available in supermarket produce departments)

1 kiwi, peeled and sliced

½ cup sliced strawberries

⅓ cup peeled, cored, and cubed pineapple

¼ cup fresh blueberries or sliced seedless green grapes

¼ cup fresh blackberries or sliced seedless red grapes

2 tablespoons fat-free aerosol whipped topping, such as Reddi-Wip

1. Position an oven rack in the center of the oven and preheat the oven to 350°F. Turn a 4-inch-wide ramekin or ovenproof bowl upside down, spray the bottom and sides with oil, and put on a baking sheet.

2. Place the crepe between 2 moistened paper towels and microwave on High (100% power) until warm and pliable, about 15 seconds. Drape over the prepared ramekin and press gently, folding up the edges of the crepe to fit the shape of the ramekin.

3. Bake until the crepe is crisp and lightly browned, 8 to 10 minutes. Let cool on the ramekin for 1 minute. Gently lift up the crepe bowl from the ramekin and put, flat side down, in a serving bowl.

4. In a small bowl, combine the kiwi, strawberries, pineapple, blueberries, and blackberries. Add the topping to the crepe bowl and spoon in the fruit. Serve.

breakfast cookies

Makes about 20 large cookies

Make these nutty cookies in advance and freeze for a quick breakfast on the go, a snack for traveling, or even as an energy bar for a long adventure. Adults like their hearty texture, but with the addition of a cup of semisweet chocolate chips, maybe the little ones in your life will enjoy them, too.

4 cups old-fashioned (rolled) oats

2 cups natural peanut butter
  or almond butter

½ cup Grade B pure maple syrup

½ cup unsweetened apple butter

1 cup mashed fully ripe bananas
  (2 large bananas)

1 cup dried cranberries

½ cup ground flaxseed (flaxseed meal)

½ cup shelled pumpkin seeds

½ cup sesame seeds

1½ teaspoons salt

1. Position the oven racks in the top third and center of the oven and preheat the oven to 325°F. Line 2 large rimmed baking sheets with parchment paper or silicone baking mats.

2. Combine all of the ingredients in the bowl of a standing heavy-duty mixer. Mix with the paddle attachment just until all the ingredients are moistened and combined into a very stiff dough.

3. Using ¼ cup for each cookie, drop the dough about 2 inches part onto the prepared baking sheets. (Or use a 2-ounce food portion scoop to transfer the dough onto the baking sheets.) Flatten the tops with your 3 middle fingers; the cookies will not spread during baking.

4. Bake, switching the position of the baking sheets from top to bottom and front to back halfway through baking, until the cookies feel firm when pressed with a fingertip and the edges are beginning to brown, about 20 minutes. Let cool on the pans for 5 minutes. Transfer the cookies to a wire cooling rack and let cool completely.

gluten-free chocolate crinkles

Makes about 7 dozen cookies

My assistant retail manager, Colleen Seiler, has a wheat intolerance, and I created this recipe so she would have something yummy to snack on while at work. Coconut flour is easy to find at supermarkets and natural food stores that carry Bob's Red Mill products.

8 tablespoons (1 stick) salted butter, cut into tablespoons

4 ounces unsweetened chocolate, finely chopped

2 teaspoons pure vanilla extract

1 teaspoon instant espresso powder

1¼ cups almond flour or finely ground slivered almonds

½ cup potato starch

½ cup white or brown rice flour

¼ cup coconut flour

¼ cup natural or Dutch-processed cocoa powder

2 teaspoons baking powder

1½ cups plus ⅓ cup granulated sugar

4 large eggs, at room temperature

1 cup (6 ounces) semisweet chocolate chips

1 cup confectioners' sugar

1. In a small saucepan, melt the butter over medium heat. Remove from the heat, add the chocolate, and let stand 2 minutes to soften. Whisk until the chocolate is melted and smooth. Whisk in the vanilla and espresso powder. Let cool until tepid.

2. In a medium bowl, whisk together the almond flour, potato starch, rice flour, coconut flour, cocoa powder, and baking powder. In a large bowl, beat 1½ cups of the granulated sugar and the eggs with an electric mixer set on high speed until the mixture is pale yellow and thick, about 3 minutes. Beat in the tepid chocolate mixture. Using a wooden spoon, gradually stir in the almond flour mixture. Stir in the chocolate chips. Cover the bowl with plastic wrap and refrigerate until the dough is chilled enough to handle easily, about 2 hours.

3. Position the oven racks in the top third and center of the oven and preheat the oven to 350°F. Line 2 large rimmed baking sheets with parchment paper or silicone baking mats.

4. Using about 1 tablespoon for each, roll the dough into balls. Put the remaining ⅓ cup granulated sugar and confectioners' sugar into 2 separate bowls. Roll each ball first in the granulated sugar, then in confectioners' sugar, and place 3 inches apart on the prepared baking sheets. Bake just until the edges of the cookies are firm and the tops are cracked, about 10 minutes. The cookies should be soft and cakey; do not overbake. Let cool on the pans for 5 minutes. Transfer the cookies to a wire cooling rack and let cool completely. Repeat with the remaining dough balls, using cooled baking sheets.

sugar-free chocolate chip cookies

Makes about 6 dozen cookies

I often get requests for sugarless baked goods. Artificial sweeteners do not suit my tastes, but I do have empathy for those who cannot eat sugar. For this sugar-free chocolate chip cookie that closely replicates Tate's original, I use maltitol, a sweetener derived from corn, sold under the brand name Steel's Nature Sweet Crystals at natural food stores and at www.steelsgourmet.com.

2 cups unbleached all-purpose flour

1 teaspoon baking soda

1 teaspoon salt

½ pound (2 sticks) salted butter, at room temperature

¾ cup Steel's Nature Sweet Brown Crystals

¾ cup Steel's Nature Sweet Crystals

2 large eggs, at room temperature

1 teaspoon pure vanilla extract

1 teaspoon water

2 cups (12 ounces) sugar-free chocolate chips

1. Position the oven racks in the top third and center of the oven and preheat the oven to 350°F. Line 2 large rimmed baking sheets with parchment paper or silicone baking mats.

2. In a medium bowl, whisk together the flour, baking soda, and salt. In a large bowl, beat the butter, Sweet Brown Crystals, and Sweet Crystals with an electric mixer set on high speed until pale and creamy, about 2 minutes. Beat in the eggs, vanilla, and water. With the mixer on low speed, mix in the flour mixture, followed by the chocolate chips.

3. Using 1 tablespoon for each cookie, drop the dough 3 inches apart onto the prepared baking sheets. The cookies will spread during baking. Let the remaining dough stand at room temperature while baking the cookies.

4. Bake, rotating the positions of the sheets from top to bottom and front to back halfway through baking, until the cookies are golden brown, about 15 minutes. Let cool on the baking sheets for 5 minutes. Transfer the cookies to a wire cooling rack and let cool completely. Repeat with the remaining dough, using cooled baking sheets.

vegan chocolate chip cookies

Makes 1½ dozen cookies

As I have said before, chocolate chip cookies are my favorite things to bake and eat. Vegan baked goods are frequently requested, so here's a cookie to satisfy the sweet tooth of my vegan customers. Some semisweet chocolate chips contain milk powder, so check the label.

1 cup instant (quick-cooking) oatmeal

½ cup whole wheat pastry flour

¼ cup coconut flour

½ teaspoon baking soda

¼ teaspoon salt

¾ cup firmly packed dark brown sugar

⅓ cup canola oil

¼ cup almond milk

2 teaspoons pure vanilla extract

½ cup vegan semisweet chocolate chips

1. Position the oven racks in the top third and center of the oven and preheat the oven to 350°F. Line 2 large rimmed baking sheets with parchment paper or silicone baking mats.

2. In a large bowl, whisk together the oatmeal, pastry flour, coconut flour, baking soda, and salt. In a medium bowl, whisk together the brown sugar, oil, almond milk, and vanilla to dissolve the sugar. Pour into the oatmeal mixture and stir until combined. Stir in the chocolate chips.

3. Using 2 tablespoons for each cookie, drop the dough 2 inches apart onto the prepared baking sheets. (Or use a 1-ounce food portion scoop to transfer the dough onto the baking sheets.) The cookies will not spread much during baking.

4. Bake the cookies for 10 minutes. Remove from the oven and gently press each cookie with the back of a soupspoon to thin the cookies and give them a more uniform look. Return the baking sheets to the oven, switching the position of the sheets from top to bottom and front to back, and bake until the cookie edges are golden brown, about 5 minutes. Let cool on the baking sheets for 5 minutes. Transfer the cookies to a wire cooling rack and let cool completely.

chapter 6

icings, frostings, & sauces

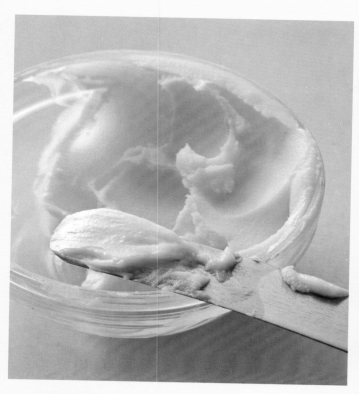

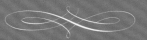

TIPS FOR ICINGS, FROSTINGS, AND SAUCES

✳ Always sift the confectioners' sugar for frostings and icings through a medium (not fine) wire sieve. It seems like a chore, but it really only takes a few seconds and makes for smoother end results.

✳ Frosting a cake is easiest if the cake is elevated a few inches off the work surface so you can see what you are doing! Professional bakers use a decorating turntable. They are easy to find at cake supply shops and online.

✳ Even if you are using a serving platter, it is a good idea to put the bottom cake layer on a cardboard baking round, which will make it easy to move the cake from one place to another. The rounds are easily found at kitchenware shops or online. In an emergency, you can always cut one from a corrugated cardboard box.

✳ To keep the frosting off the serving platter, slip 3 or 4 strips of waxed paper under the bottom cake layer. After frosting, slide out the strips. You will only have to do a very light touch-up, if any.

✳ An offset metal icing spatula is a good tool for applying frosting, but I have also used a table knife. Serious bakers have a large spatula for frosting layer cakes and a small one for cupcakes.

aunt betty's flour icing

Makes enough for one 9-inch layer cake

Recently I ran into my cousin Peggy, and the conversation turned to her Mom's chocolate cake with marshmallow icing. She smiled and said, "That wasn't marshmallow. It was her flour icing." Soon after, she gave me the recipe. It sounds strange, but it is just as I remember it—light and fluffy, not too sweet or too rich. It can be refrigerated for a day or two, brought to room temperature, and whipped back to perfection. If you love chocolate cake with vanilla icing as I do (see page 166 for one of my favorites), trust me on this one. My cake decorator, Debbie Rowe, makes this with brown sugar instead of granulated, and it is outstanding!

¼ cup plus 2 tablespoons unbleached all-purpose flour

1½ cups milk

¾ pound (3 sticks) unsalted butter, cut into tablespoons, at cool room temperature (not too soft)

1½ cups sugar

1 tablespoon pure vanilla extract

1. Put the flour in a small saucepan and gradually whisk in the milk until smooth. Bring to a boil over medium heat, whisking constantly, then cook until thick and smooth, still whisking, about 30 seconds. Transfer to a small bowl and press plastic wrap directly against the surface of the flour mixture. Let cool completely. (The flour mixture can be made up to 1 day ahead, cooled, and refrigerated.)

2. In a large bowl, beat the butter and sugar with an electric mixer set on high speed until very light and fluffy, about 4 minutes. Gradually beat in the flour mixture and continue beating until the icing is light and fluffy again, about 1 minute. Beat in the vanilla. (The icing can be made up to 2 days ahead, covered tightly and refrigerated. Let stand at room temperature for 1 hour, and beat with an electric mixer set on high speed to fluff it up again before using.)

"church lady" vanilla icing

Makes enough for one 9-inch layer cake

This icing is the sweet, thick kind that you might recall from church functions such as bake sales, rummage fairs, and coffee hours. It frosts cakes in ivory swirls.

½ pound (2 sticks) salted butter, at room temperature

5 cups (1¼ pounds) confectioners' sugar, sifted

1 tablespoon pure vanilla extract

About ¾ cup heavy cream

1. In a large bowl, beat the butter with an electric mixer set on high speed until creamy, about 1 minute. With the mixer on low speed, beat in the confectioners' sugar, 1 cup at a time, beating well after each addition and scraping down the sides of the bowl as needed. Beat in the vanilla. Beat in enough of the heavy cream, 1 tablespoon at a time, to give the icing the consistency you prefer. Then beat with the mixer on high speed until light and fluffy, about 1 minute more.

fluffy vanilla icing

Makes enough for one 9-inch layer cake

Here is the soft icing that looks like it came out of a fifties diner. It is actually much less sweet than other icings, and it provides a perfect color and flavor contrast to chocolate layer cake. The icing is best served the day it is made.

1 cup sugar

⅓ cup water

¼ teaspoon cream of tartar

2 large egg whites, at room temperature

1 teaspoon pure vanilla extract

1. In a small saucepan, bring the sugar, water, and cream of tartar to a full boil over medium heat, stirring just until the sugar dissolves.

2. Meanwhile, in a medium bowl, using an electric mixer set on high speed, beat the egg whites until they form soft peaks. Remove the syrup from the heat. With the mixer running, slowly add the hot syrup in a thin, steady stream, taking care to avoid the whirling beaters. Continue beating until the icing is fluffy, cooled, and spreadable, about 5 minutes. Beat in the vanilla. Use immediately, frosting the cake with a metal icing spatula, and using the spatula to create swirls.

Pink Fluffy Icing: Beat 1 to 2 tablespoons of the juice from a jar of maraschino cherries into the icing with the vanilla.

cream cheese icing

Makes enough for one 9-inch layer cake

Cream cheese icing goes well with more than just carrot cake. Try it on chocolate cake, yellow cake, or your favorite recipe. The ginger variation is excellent with the Beet and Rhubarb Cake on page 163.

1 pound cream cheese,
  at room temperature

8 tablespoons (1 stick) salted butter,
  at room temperature

2½ cups confectioners' sugar, sifted

2 teaspoons pure vanilla extract

1. In a large bowl, beat the cream cheese and butter with an electric mixer set on high speed until creamy, about 1 minute. Gradually beat in the confectioners' sugar, beating well after each addition and scraping down the sides of the bowl as needed. Beat in the vanilla. If you prefer a thick and creamy texture, use immediately. For a lighter, fluffier icing, beat for 1 to 2 minutes longer. If the icing seems too thin, refrigerate to chill slightly before using.

Ginger Cream Cheese Icing: Yes, this icing won't be smooth, but the lumps will be delicious. Beat ½ cup minced crystallized ginger into the finished icing.

White Chocolate Cream Cheese Icing: The white chocolate adds a vanilla flavor to the icing. Melt 8 ounces white chocolate, finely chopped, as directed on page 46; let cool until tepid but still fluid. Use only 2 cups confectioners' sugar. Beat in the white chocolate after the confectioner's sugar.

caramel icing

Makes enough for one 8- to 9-inch layer cake

What could be better than sweet caramel icing dripping down the sides of your cake? But this icing can be temperamental. When it cools, it firms up, so use while it is still warm.

1½ cups firmly packed dark brown sugar

1 cup heavy cream

2 tablespoons salted butter

2 tablespoons Grade B pure maple syrup

1. In a deep heavy-bottomed medium saucepan, combine the brown sugar and cream. Attach a candy thermometer to the pan and bring to a boil over medium-high heat, stirring constantly; take care that the mixture doesn't boil over. Boil, stirring occasionally, brushing down any sugar crystals that form on the inside of the saucepan with a natural bristle brush dipped in cold water, until it reaches the soft ball stage (236°F), about 15 minutes. Remove from the heat. Stir in the butter and maple syrup and let stand until the icing cools to 110°F, about 20 minutes.

2. Using a wire whisk, beat the icing until thick enough to spread. Use immediately.

chocolate fudge icing

Makes enough for one 9-inch layer cake

We have used this icing for over thirty years at the Bake Shop. It is very thick, dense, fudgy, and sweet. My niece Kara has requested this icing on a yellow cake for every birthday, and she is now twenty-four!

6 ounces unsweetened chocolate, finely chopped

6 ounces cream cheese, at room temperature

3 tablespoons salted butter, at room temperature

2 teaspoons pure vanilla extract

5½ cups (1½ pounds) confectioners' sugar, sifted

⅓ cup plus 1 tablespoon milk

3 tablespoons light corn syrup

Pinch of salt

1. Put the chocolate in a microwave-safe bowl and heat at Medium (50% power), stirring at 30-second intervals, until the chocolate is melted and smooth, about 2 minutes. Let cool until tepid but fluid.

2. In a large bowl, beat the cream cheese and butter with an electric mixer set on high speed until combined, about 1 minute. Beat in the vanilla. With the mixer on low speed, beat in the confectioners' sugar, 1 cup at a time, beating well after each addition and scraping down the sides of the bowl as needed. Add the milk, corn syrup, and salt and beat with the mixer on low speed, scraping down the sides of the bowl as needed, until smooth and fluffy. Beat in the cooled chocolate and mix well.

milk chocolate mocha frosting

Makes enough for one 9-inch double-layer cake

This icing is quick, smooth, and creamy. I love it on the Chocolate Chip Layer Cake on page 164. The mocha flavor is very mild and gives just the right touch to the cake. Even though it uses milk chocolate, it is not as sweet as you may think. I usually choose dark chocolate over milk chocolate, but this frosting is fantastic!

1½ pounds high-quality milk chocolate, finely chopped

3½ cups heavy cream

6 tablespoons (¾ stick) unsalted butter, cut into ½-inch cubes

2 tablespoons instant espresso powder

2 teaspoons pure vanilla extract

1. Put the chocolate in a medium heatproof bowl. Bring the cream to a boil in a medium saucepan over medium heat, taking care that it doesn't boil over. Remove from the heat, add the butter, espresso powder, and vanilla, and stir until the butter melts. Pour over the milk chocolate. Let stand until the chocolate softens, about 1 minute.

2. Whisk until the chocolate is completely melted and smooth. Cover the bowl with plastic wrap. Refrigerate until the mixture is as thick as chocolate pudding, about 2 hours.

3. Beat the chocolate mixture with an electric mixer set on high speed, just until it becomes lighter in color and spreadable, about 10 seconds. Be very careful not to overbeat, or it will separate. (In that case, melt the mixture in a stainless-steel bowl set over a saucepan of simmering water. Cover and refrigerate until thickened, and try again.)

whipped cream

Makes about 2 cups

It takes only a few minutes to whip cream, and for such minimal effort, the flavor and texture of the real thing can't be beat. If you overwhip heavy cream (it will look pale yellow, not white), beat in a little more cream to loosen it and it will be fine. (If you don't have extra cream on hand, try plain yogurt or sour cream.)

  1 cup heavy cream
  2 tablespoons sugar
  1 teaspoon pure vanilla extract

In a medium bowl, whip the cream, sugar, and vanilla with an electric mixer set on high speed just until stiff peaks begin to form. (Better yet: Measure the cream, sugar, and vanilla into a 1-quart glass measuring cup. Whip the cream with a hand-held mixer right in the cup. You will have one less bowl to wash.) A lighter texture is better than one that is too stiff. Cover with plastic wrap and refrigerate until ready to serve, up to 1 day. If the cream separates, just whisk to return to the proper consistency.

Maple Whipped Cream: Substitute 2 tablespoons Grade B pure maple syrup for the sugar.

Baileys Whipped Cream: Add 2 tablespoons Irish whisky cream liqueur, such as Baileys, to the cream mixture.

nutella whipped cream

Makes about 4½ cups

Nutella takes whipped cream to another place! I use this often as a frosting for layer cake. If you are making this for the Brownie Pie on page 71, or to dollop alongside a slice of tea cake, make half a batch.

2 cups heavy cream
1 cup Nutella or other chocolate-hazelnut spread

1. In a small saucepan, bring the cream to a boil over medium heat, being sure it doesn't boil over. Remove from the heat, add the Nutella, and whisk until smooth. Pour into a heat-proof bowl and let stand until tepid. Cover with plastic wrap and refrigerate until chilled, at least 2 hours, or up to 1 day.

2. Whip the cream mixture with an electric mixer set on high speed until it is as thick as you like. If using it for a frosting, whip until stiff peaks form.

raspberry coulis

Makes about 1 cup

In French cuisine, coulis (koo-LEE) is a thick sauce made from a puree of fruit or, sometimes, vegetables. Raspberry coulis has a lot of uses, and it is an easy way to add bright magenta color and tart berry flavor to a simple dessert.

2 cups fresh or individually quick frozen (IQF) raspberries
⅓ cup sugar
1 tablespoon water

1. In a small saucepan, cook the raspberries, sugar, and water over medium-low heat, stirring often, until the raspberries are very soft and the juices have thickened slightly, about 10 minutes.

2. Pour into a fine wire sieve set over a bowl. Using a rubber spatula, rub the coulis through the sieve; discard the seeds in the sieve. Refrigerate until ready to serve.

acknowledgments

I would like to express my heartfelt gratitude to my local community of Southampton, Long Island, and to all my loyal customers who continue to enrich my life and who share their lives with me.

I am forever grateful to so many in my life, but a special thank you goes out to the following people that made this book come alive:

Tate's Bake Shop would never be the national success it is without the direction and dedication of my business manager, Michael Naimy. Every day, I am thankful that we met and chose to work together.

To my amazing staff at both retail and wholesale levels, who keep the passion, joy, and excitement in every day—thank you for your commitment and hard work.

To my husband, Zvi Friedman, for his brilliant engineering to keep everything growing, running, and held together. You are always proud and supportive of me.

To my son, Justin Friedman, for his constructive opinions and insight, and to his college roommates for eating up all my experiments and always offering their honest critiques.

To my inspiring Mom and Dad (Tate), for teaching me to share with everyone and to keep an open door and an open heart.

To Rick Rodgers, the editor of this book, who never stopped amazing me with his eye for detail, his knowledge and expertise in baking, and his genuine desire to make this book the very best it could be. You taught me a lot.

To Barbara Scott-Goodman, for her creative direction that brought my recipes, lifestyle, and the bakeshop, to life in these pages.

To Alexandra Rowley, for enhancing my baked goods with her photography. Her down-to-earth style and attitude made our business meetings fun and stress free. At the end of each photo session, I was in awe.

To Liza Jernow, our food stylist, who can make the simplest treat look like a work of art. I enjoyed her skill, calmness, and ability to make the most common items look spectacular.

To Pamela Duncan Silver, our prop designer, who always knew the perfect plate, fork, or background to present my baked goods beautifully.

To Judith Sutton, the copy editor, for catching the small details we missed.

To Suzanne Fass, the proofreader for making sure everything was perfect in the end.

To Tony Lopez, for helping me present my thoughts in writing much better than I could by myself.

To Carla Glasser, for always pushing me forward with enthusiasm and energy; I will always be grateful.

To all my friends and family who contributed, tasted, and critiqued recipes—without you I wouldn't love baking as much as I do.

index